D0663830

LEARN MORE to EARN MORE

Med Serif

Published by arrangement with Frederick Fell Publishers Inc.

To L. T. White
who inspired this book
and to my three M's,
Marylin, Mike, and Missy,
who put up with the many hours
I spent writing it, offering
only encouragement.

How to Succeed in Business by Trying

In mid-1958, a fascinating new frontier was opened for me by L. T. White, then Vice President of Cities Service Petroleum, a subsidiary of the Cities Service Company. L. T. was, you could say, pioneering in a vast new area—big business assistance to small business.

Working with him to do more than offer just the normal advertising, promotion, and accounting assistance, we sought to help men and women improve their managerial abilities.

In our research, we soon saw that even the best executive could easily become completely tied up in a mass of detail. The performance of the modern executive—whether owner, hired manager, or employee—is the cornerstone for the success of a business in our highly competitive society. Too many men and women fail to achieve complete success because they do not operate at the fullest efficiency at all times.

Believing that executives could grow in ability by learning to be more effective, we began trying to help them do a better job of self-management. We wrote articles, prepared booklets, gave speeches, and taught classes. Our findings proved of equal value and interest to the owners of businesses and to the executives of large and small companies.

This is a field which seems to have no end. Every time I talk to someone, new subjects are suggested. Basically, however, they all fall into three specific areas —improving self-efficiency, human relations with others, and living a fuller personal life.

In this book I've tried to answer many of the questions and to offer solutions to problems that are faced by busy men and women. I offer thanks to Cities Service for both the opportunity to explore this fascinating field and for permission to utilize some of our research in the writing of this book.

MED SERIF

CONTENTS

Managing Yourself

1

The MAN in MANagement

How often have you felt there just weren't enough hours in the day to meet all the demands your business or your job makes of you? I doubt that government will ever legislate a 28-hour day into existence, so it's up to you to become more effective in your everyday work.

In today's tightly competitive business world this is especially true. Success comes to the organization which is just a little bit better than its competition. In most cases that slight edge lies not in machinery, or even products. It lies in the men running the business.

Modern medicine hasn't yet found a pill that will make you a better "self"-manager. But there are things you can do. In a large sense, this book will point out objectives and methods for reaching the peak in self-efficiency.

There Is a Secret

Successful men have found the secret of "getting on top of their jobs." Their secret, if you want to call it that, is threefold:

1. You must want to work at top efficiency.
2. You must organize yourself.
3. Once you've stopped "spinning your wheels," you must discipline yourself to stick to your new-found efficiency.

An executive's job is basic. You must see opportunity. You must plan. You must organize. You must control. You must improve and change course whenever necessary.

The ease and speed with which you accomplish these tasks depends upon a combination of factors, all basically within you. Your success is based on your innate abilities, your acquired skills, your efficiency, health and vigor, your foresight, and your desire to succeed.

No matter what your job or your business, you are probably well organized to meet mechanical breakdowns or similar headaches. Preventive maintenance would probably have caught any problems at their start. Friction between people or departments is quickly eliminated.

Yet, when it comes to operating at maximum efficiency, we are apt to find the job too often runs us. The answer is simple. Too many managers fail to manage themselves. As a result, they barely limp along at half or less efficiency.

The Briefcase Every Night

The son of a large multistate oil-distributor friend is a perfect example. He told me, "When I took the business over from Dad three years ago, I was able to run it and I still had time for my family, my golf, and the other things we enjoyed. Now, I lug the briefcase home just about every night. Nothing I do seems to help. I never seem to get caught up. What's wrong?"

I spent the next few days following him around his office and his bulk plants. It didn't take long to spot just what had gone wrong.

My friend had left his son a solid enterprise. The boy had learned his lessons well and had added new innovations and equipment. He spent a good deal of time talking to men in the oil and other businesses. He listened and questioned his suppliers and his bankers. His business flourished.

He gave everything his personal touch. Today, he was still trying to keep his fingers in every pie. The business had more than tripled in size, but he still had only two hands, two feet, two eyes, one brain, and the same twenty-four hours a day he had before.

I spelled out bluntly the trouble as I saw it. "You are wasting too much time on details, and too little time actually doing your job—managing."

He readily saw this and agreed. But how was he to become more effective on the job?

Actually he had taken the first step when he admitted that he had tied his hands with red tape and details. He had begun to organize himself. Only self-management would make him more effective in his work.

Managing vs. Operating

The transition from operating a business or a job to managing is a mental one. It's been said there are four steps:

1. Realize that you can't do all the work yourself.
2. Admit that you can't make every decision. You must trust others to make some for you.
3. Recognize the importance of planning.
4. Continually check your progress.

It's not easy to manage yourself. Some of us are too tired to make the effort. Others are indifferent and content to let things just roll along. A few may be too lazy to try. But if you were to weigh the results of self-organization, you would quickly see the solid gold advantages that would fall to you. Here are six of the more prominent advantages:

1. You do more, and what you accomplish is better.
2. You can set goals for yourself
3. You can continually check to see if you are on course.
4. You can save time.
5. You eliminate habits that bring ulcers and sleepless nights.
6. You do a better job of leading and inspiring others.

Self-Discipline Is the Key

Organization and operating efficiency, like charity, should begin at home. Ask yourself honestly if you are now performing at 100 per cent efficiency every minute of your working day. If you are not, the answer is self-discipline. You must decide that you and only you will be boss. Distractions are ruled out. You must see to it that you complete your work in the fastest possible time, without any wasted energy.

Good planning starts with the formulation of a schedule. Keep a careful record of your activities over a period of several weeks. Be sure to note the jobs you've failed to find time for, as well as those you completed.

Chapter 2 will fully discuss the management of time and tell you how to analyze your time. For our purposes here, we should emphasize that a careful analysis of your working time is essential. It will reveal that certain activities are probably done on a regular basis. Others happen only occasionally. One suggestion is to group your different activities according to the people you work with.

A second suggestion is to group your tasks according to the nature of the work. Similar activities should be made to link up. Your work on one project may be useful on another job. For example, planning and decision-making could be done right after the morning mail is read. Or you might hold it for next to the last, until just before you plan your next day's activities.

In a nutshell, your different tasks should fall into a logical order, based on their relative importance. With first preference given important jobs, the routine will be taken care of during spare time..

Many successful executives handle these routine jobs during their spare time. It is amazing how much time can be wasted traveling to or from work, waiting to see clients, or sitting at your desk waiting for a late caller. This is the time to look over papers, to sign mail, to read your business publications.

Deferred business must be scheduled ahead and some tool, such as a "tickler" file, used to call it to mind in plenty of time for careful thought and action. I've found a handy booklet is one that provides spaces for the following: date job acknowledged; job description; date job is due; date job completed, or dropped, or transferred. Another valuable item, especially so in these days of close tax accounting, is a spiral-bound calendar book. Get one that lists every day of the month. List your appointments on each day, and also special projects handled. This becomes an excellent diary of your activities throughout the year.

In all this talk of planning, care should be taken to allow for handling of any emergencies or problems that might arise.

In Chapter 2 we'll see how to break up our day into time-work blocks. You simply set up a schedule and manage yourself so that you stick to this schedule. A major advantage of such a schedule is that it points out poor use of time.

The "Too Busy" Bosses

Killing the working day seems to be the favorite hobby of many executives at all levels. Several years ago the United States Small Business Administration identified some of these "Busy, Busy Bosses." They were called:

"*The Detail-Hugger:* Hardly a day passes without his presence distracting the mailroom clerk ('Have you got enough stamps'), the secretaries ('How do you put a new ribbon on that new machine'). He is also terribly interested in the amount of string used for packages and the amount of gas used by the company trucks.

"*The Conference Caller:* This type won't let anyone order a dozen paper cups without the trappings of a time-killing executive summit meeting. He likes to hear his own voice, even if no one else does.

"*The Dream Merchant:* He kills time dreaming (and worse luck, talking) about what he's going to do tomorrow, and so he never has time to do anything today.

"*The Kibitzer:* Killing his day is not a problem. He just does it by looking over everybody's shoulder, and dropping in on departments 'Just to see how things are going.'

"*The One-Track Manager:* Charlie-One-Track loves business statistics. Figures fascinate him, and he spends the day poring over them, while decisions that have to be made just wait.

"*The Overflowing-Desk Man:* Killing the day is no problem for this man. He wastes time signing innumerable notes, memos, requisitions and other interoffice trivia.

"*The Genius:* He knows everybody's job so much better than the man doing it that he spends most of his time managing everyone's time and effort . . . but never his own.

"*The Open Door Man:* My door (this executive announces proudly) is open to everybody at all times. The idea is fine, but the result is disastrous. His employees take up most of his day with trivial questions that they could figure out for themselves if the boss hadn't given them a green light to kill his day."

Naturally, not all men and women fall into one or another of these categories. The really successful ones spend their time managing, controlling, planning and directing the work of others.

Stick to Your Schedule

Once you have analyzed what must be done and prepared a schedule, you must stick to this plan of organization. Everything should be completed in the time period allotted. This schedule serves three purposes:

1. It assures that a job will be completed in the allotted time with the desired results.
2. It permits you to check your own progress.
3. If you've gone astray, you'll know where and when, and you can take the necessary action.

What's Actually Your Job

You can help organize yourself if you carefully reappraise what is actually expected of you. The Small Business Administration suggests that many men and women could better organize themselves if they were to follow this simple blueprint for executive thought and action:

1. Realize that your business, or any business, becomes more complex as it grows. It may require the skills and abilities of such experts as accountants, lawyers, management consultants, as well as the capable men in your own organization.

2. Realize that your job is to see your business as a whole. The job of these hired and salaried experts is to provide special knowledge.

3. Your function is to supply top policy.

4. Your purpose is to lead, inspire, direct.

5. Never stop re-evaluating your job. Ask yourself daily whether you are doing all you should. Are you neglecting some other tasks, or doing some that should better be left to others?

6. Each day set aside some time to think. Close your door and make sure no one interrupts you. Take all the time you need. On some days it may only be a few minutes. Other days may require hours.

7. Each day set aside some time to make plans for the future.

8. Each day make certain that you have taken care of the important things before you tackle anything else.

9. Each day be sure to do all the tasks you should be doing, even the unpleasant ones. Perhaps the paper work is unpleasant and you'd rather be talking to a favorite customer. To do things you dislike means that you have disciplined yourself.

10. Each day do some "on-the-job" coaching. That means training your assistants to help you and to do their own jobs at a better level of efficiency.

11. Each day remember that you are working with friends. A smile and a pleasant word can often accomplish the impossible.

12. At the end of each day sit back and think about the tasks you worked on. Ask yourself if you could have left some undone and completed others. Were there important tasks left undone? Was time wasted on pleasant work while less appealing, but more important, jobs were left undone?

To sum it all up, only organization can put you on the road to complete efficiency and job satisfaction. With organization, you know what goals you want to reach and, with careful thought, just how you are going to get there.

Actually, the first steps for self-organization are the ones we will describe later in this book to help us make decisions. These are:

1. Clearly define your problem. In this case it is organizing to meet a specific problem.
2. Carefully analyze all pertinent aspects of the problem.
3. Develop alternative solutions for the problem.
4. Select the one best solution.
5. Translate your decision into action.

We need add only a schedule to be adhered to, and the management action of changing course if our first solution proves unsuitable.

Use All Available Aids

Self-management does demand more than just a carefully planned schedule. You must make the fullest use of all available tools at your disposal. These include your own body, your mind, and a wide variety of physical equipment.

Today's business world exacts a heavy toll of our nervous systems and our bodies. Later in this book we'll discuss working under tension and maintaining our health.

There are too many ways to waste your valuable energy. You can waste a substantial amount of time by acquiring poor habits of concentration, of planning, or even of thinking.

You can waste your time because you've let bad

eating and sleeping habits drain away your energy. Failure to control your emotions will handcuff the hands of many men and women. The failure to use properly the tools at hand such as the telephone or your desk will also cause you to waste time.

There is an answer for stopping these energy leaks. It is this self-discipline we've already mentioned. You must decide that you will be boss, that you want to complete your work in the fastest time, without wasted energy.

Your own mind is the most important asset you have in achieving self-organization. Your mind can be made an important ally if you try to concentrate on improving three groups or areas of your mental activities:

1. Improve your ability to concentrate. One tip here: Keep distractions to a minimum.
2. Continually increase your knowledge so you can more readily analyze ideas and problems and make the right decision.
3. Your memory is a muscle. Exercise it so you are able to retain and recall information when it is needed.

Each of these mental abilities can be developed to the highest degree. Watch others work. Analyze your own working habits. Study and hold fast to the desire to improve. Make resolutions to overcome bad habits, and see that you keep these resolutions. You can replace bad habits with good ones because all patterns of behavior have to be learned, and you can guide and control your learning.

The Physical Aids

Beyond your mind and your body there are certain physical tools to use. Let's start simply. How many of you carry a pencil and a small note pad? Don't trust to memory. Write everything down. The facts or figures you forget can spell the difference between profit and loss.

When I first began to travel as a business magazine editor some years ago, it seemed easy to remember all requests that were made of me. After several years and many conventions, I sat down at my desk on a Monday morning after one convention and looked at the cards I had collected. Each represented a request. But who wanted reprints? Who had asked me to make a convention speech? Which operation had the makings of a good feature article? My mind was a complete blank.

Since that day I've always taken notes. Perhaps too many notes, but when I make a promise, I know I'll fulfill it.

Time is definitely essential for following a schedule. It may seem silly to say this, but own and carry a good watch.

An efficient office and desk are other important crutches to the busy executive. They are your base of operations. They can save time and steps and speed the flow of work. Both your desk and office require careful planning. Pull out any drawer in your desk. Is it really organized, or do you have to shuffle through an assortment of cards, papers, envelopes, and paperclips?

Here are three rules for efficient office and desk organization:

1. Locate the most used furniture and equipment as close as possible. If you do a lot of figuring, have a calculator in your office. Don't force yourself to walk out to find one that someone else may be using.

2. Make the office as attractive as possible, but do not let it distract you. Colors should be restful and cheerful. Pictures should be of your choice but should fit into the overall scheme.

3. Your desk should hold only immediately usable work and necessary supplies. Papers belong in their proper files. Reminders such as addresses, phone numbers, and other similar information may be kept either in a box on your desk or in a drawer.

The human element in the office may be the most important. When you've arrived at the level to either share a secretary or to have your own, she should be carefully trained. It will be her responsibility to protect you from unnecessary callers, to remind you of pending projects, and to do a million other things. We'll discuss more completely the role of this vital young lady in Chapter 4.

Getting on top of your job will help you accomplish your work in far fewer hours and in a more accurate and efficient manner. It will assure you that you are making the fullest use of your God-given talents. When you achieve this pinnacle, success will have more than monetary value. You will have achieved a sense of tremendous satisfaction for a job well done.

2

How to Manage Your Time

Successful men have learned how to make time work for them. They have also proved that others can learn how to make the most out of each working day.

When you achieve this peak, you need no longer fear those Friday or Saturday afternoons that used to close out a week—with a pile of work left undone. Time has become your servant. No longer are you a time-killer.

There are four steps to taking over full control of the all too few working hours you have. These steps are:

1. You must measure your time.
2. You must find where you waste time.
3. You must plan the most effective use of your hours.
4. You must continually look for short cuts and ways to save time.

How to Measure Time

Preparation of a timetable calls first for analysis of all of your activities. Here you carefully analyze not only the jobs you've completed, but also those for which you failed to find time.

Looking back you'll quickly find that certain activities are regularly repeated. Others are faced only occasionally. The following Analysis Form will help you prepare a profile of your activities.

	Daily		Weekly							Monthly			
ctivity	AM	PM	M	T	W	T	F	S	S	1 Week	2 Week	3 Week	4 Week

Each daily activity should be checked in the morning or afternoon period in which it is handled. Weekly jobs should be checked by the day the work is done. Each monthly job should be checked in the week the work is normally done. If an activity is done more than once, check the appropriate squares.

A second method for analyzing time provides an actual measurement of the time spent in each activity. This analysis can be done with a simple sheet of ruled paper. Start by putting the hour you begin work on the top line at the left. On the second line put the next quarter hour. On the third line the next quarter hour, etc., continuing until you reach the end of your working day. For example, if you start at 8 A.M., put that on the top line; 8:15 on the second line, and so on.

Now draw lines down the page. This separates the sheet into columns. Write at the top of each column the things you do. For instance, you might write at the head of one column "Reading Mail." "Dictation" might head a second column. A third could be "Visiting Customers." List everything that your job entails.

Time	*Activities*						
	Reading Mail	Dictation	Sales Calls	Writing Reports	Sales Meetings	Waiting	Travel
8:00							
8:15							
8:30							
etc.							

When you have the form made, sit down at the end of the first day. Think back through the hours of the day and put checkmarks under the things you did. Go down the page and account for every quarter-hour.

When you count the marks in each column, you'll be able to see, at a glance, what proportion of your time was spent at each activity. When you add up the checkmarks, you've measured your time.

After you've measured your time, carefully analyze your activities with this thought uppermost in your mind: Am I allocating the proper time to my different tasks? If the unimportant seem to take too much time, rearranging just a few key jobs will often make a tremendous difference in your rate of efficiency.

In other words . . . "Work Smarter, Not Harder."

Scheduling Your Time

Each person must find the one best way to manage the use of his time. One of the most used and simplest techniques is to sit down on a Sunday night and carefully list everything you want to do during the coming week. It is wise to list these projects by day, with the most important tasks heading each daily list.

Keep this list in front of you throughout the week. Everytime a job is completed, you've earned the right to scratch it off your list. Those uncompleted jobs will begin to haunt you, as the list sits on your desk or burns a hole in your pocket.

Some men and women prefer to make out their checklists each night for the coming day. Their aim is to complete each day's assigned work before closing the calendar on that day. It becomes a matter of pride to go home with all scheduled work accomplished.

When the checklist is prepared is unimportant. The important thing is to get into the habit of thinking out a schedule.

In Chapter 1 we suggested that you segregate your activities according to importance and by linking with other tasks that logically come together. When this is done, you'll often find that information developed, or work you've completed on one project can be utilized as background material for another project.

I had a personal example of this some time ago. My company donated my time so that I could prepare a booklet on "Developing An Assistant" for the United States Small Business Administration. The research I did for this project was utilized later when I developed a sales management series as part of our dealer-relations activities. You'll find this material as the basis of Chapter 17.

It is a good rule to try to make one minute do the work of two by utilizing your efforts to produce information or material that can be used in more than one way.

Budgeting Activities

Budgeting your time simply means breaking down your workday into the time you'll spend on each activity. The two simple systems for analyzing time we illustrated earlier in this chapter should help you do this.

There are just two ways to make the most of your time. One is to eliminate things that don't have to be done. The other is to work as hard as possible on the essential activities that are left.

Once you've analyzed your workday to separate the essential from the unessential tasks, the next step is to decide which jobs must be given a regular place on your schedule, and which should be handled during a free or open period.

Too many men and women waste time by doing first the jobs they like or find easiest. This is poor management. The sales manager who sells is not really a manager. He sells simply because he wants to get the job done, or because he'd rather do it himself. A good manager or supervisor supresses his other interests and concentrates solely on his job—building a stronger business. He hires workers and delegates the work. Remember, one of the prime rules of management is that the lowest-paid individual qualified to do a job is given the assignment.

Your own analysis will quickly show if the odds and ends and trifles have been eating up your time. Concentrating on the really important work will become a habit. The simple checklist made out once a month or every night will quickly put the spotlight on those essential jobs that must have priority.

How important is it to get rid of the unessentials? Just stop for a moment to see what your wasted time is actually costing you.

When You Earn	*Every Hour Costs You*	*Every Minute Costs You*	*In One Year, One Wasted Hour Costs You*
$ 5,000	$ 2.56	.042¢	$ 627
10,000	5.12	.084¢	1,254
15,000	7.68	.126¢	1,881
20,000	10.24	.168¢	2,508
25,000	12.80	.210¢	3,133

* Based on 244 eight-hour work days a year.

So you see, the time you possess is worth a great deal. Don't spend it in foolish pursuits.

Gaining More Time

Is it possible to add more minutes or even hours to a day? The answer is *yes* if you will use the secret ingredient—management. More specifically, in this case, the management of your time.

The first step is to understand that your time is worth money. That preceding chart will emphatically point this out. You must also accept the fact that you can only do a better job when you are willing to make an effort.

The next logical step is to set goals for yourself. You may wish to visit more customers, dictate more letters, read more reports or books, or have more time for your family, or to play golf. You must set goals, and you must make every effort to stay right on the path toward these targets.

One automobile salesman I know is successful because he always has prospects in some stage of being ready to be "closed." His secret is to continually find new prospects—"hot" prospects. He makes it his every-day business to mail out at least five postcards to new names, to make at least five phone calls to those he's already contacted or sold, and to make five personal calls on those just about ready to close.

He does all this while taking his turn on the sales floor. How does he do it? He has set his personal daily goals of five for each category and he keeps a regular score on his desk pad. He has no spare minutes, because when a lull comes along, he is making a phone call, writing a card, or driving off to a demonstration.

Is he a success? Ask his boss.

You can set goals for any task. Some years ago, while working for a business magazine, I was writing my thesis for a master's degree. After spending the five weekdays over a hot typewriter, I did not look forward to writing at night or on weekends.

I finally challenged myself to do five pages a night and twenty pages each Saturday and Sunday until the project was completed. My wife agreed to help. Each night I put five paperclips in a coffee cup on one side of the table. As I finished each page, I took one clip out of the cup. Every so often my wife would stop by to check my progress. When the cup had been emptied of four of the clips, she was to put up the coffee and start to make me a sandwich or cut a piece of pie. The coffee would be poured into the empty cup when the last clip was removed.

The first night my wife gave up and went to bed after waiting an hour past our regular bedtime. The second night I made it, but about thirty minutes late. The third day I hit my goal with a little time to spare. From then on I hit my goal every night.

Pinpointing Your Goals

It is wise to pinpoint your goals. A lot of people waste time and energy simply because they do not have a clear idea of what they want or are supposed to do.

This is the place where the five-step program for self-organization described in Chapter 1 comes in handy. Before you begin any job, mentally run it through the following five steps:

1. Define your problem as clearly as possible.
2. Carefully analyze all pertinent aspects.
3. Develop alternative solutions.
4. Select the one best solution.
5. Translate your decision into action.

Setting Realistic Deadlines

Any timetable you set for yourself should be a realistic one. Before you actually set your deadlines, you must allow yourself sufficient time to gather and analyze all pertinent facts and to contact all others who are involved in the project in any way.

You must also gather any tools or supplies that the job may require. If you don't prepare yourself, you may waste a lot of valuable time every instance you have to stop to get a fact book, or even paper, or a typewriter ribbon.

Allow time for the unexpected. Sickness, emergencies, unexpected visitors, even a loss of energy as the day draws to a close will cause wasteful delays. If the delays fail to occur, you'll look just that much better because you finished the job early.

See if you can beat the deadlines you set. This provides an extra incentive and may actually increase your efficiency. Tests show that the rapid worker is often more accurate than the slower one. This might be because the rapid worker is like an automobile driver. He tries out different speeds of work. When he finds the one at which he is most efficient, he continues along at that pace. The slow worker may never really discover what he can do.

How to Acquire More Time

You can acquire more time. Yes—time, like any other commodity, can be bought, it can be manufactured, and it can even be stored. You can gain time in various ways, so here are some hints:

1. Get up fifteen minutes earlier to avoid the morning rush and also streamline your procedure for getting out of your home. You can do this by keeping your personal items grouped together, ready for use. It's also a help to decide the night before what to wear and to have your clothes laid out. You will arrive at work feeling much more relaxed when you eliminate morning fumbling.

2. Increase your reading and writing skills. Wouldn't it be wonderful to read all those publica-

tions and reports and have them flow across your desk almost as soon as they arrive? You can learn to increase your reading speed. In like manner, you can learn to write better reports, letters, and memos. You'll see how this is done in Chapters 5 and 14. These skills will save you much time.

3. Develop the habit of making good notes. Store your ideas, facts, figures, and bits of information. Keep reference files and tickler files to guide you in your everyday activities. The good note-taker finds that he can drop even the biggest problems and come back later to pick up the threads without wasting time trying to remember facts.

Make it a habit to prepare notes, either during or immediately after meetings or important conversations. Get the facts and decisions made down on paper while they are still fresh in your mind. This saves time and avoids misunderstandings.

4. Be decisive and act fast. This prevents strangulation by the loose ends. For instance, answer your correspondence at once and you will be rid of almost 95 per cent of it. You can then concentrate on the special or creative problems involved in the other 5 per cent.

Some executives I know dictate even though all the facts are not yet available. They leave a blank space for their secretaries to insert the needed information when it becomes available. If they must leave a loose end, they specify who is to do what, when. One big advantage here is that you do not have to come back to a task and spend a great deal of time refreshing your memory.

5. Control your telephone. This fine invention

saves you time-consuming travel. Instead of "legging" it down to see somebody, pick up the phone. It is a fast way of getting information, of checking facts, or for giving instructions.

But this same telephone can become a monster if you allow yourself to be drawn into time-wasting bull sessions. Get your wife out of the habit of calling you for every little thing. Generally her worries or conversation can wait until you get home. And cut out any nonessential phone calls that you may have gotten into the habit of making.

Before you make a business call, make certain you have everything you need at hand—pencil, note paper, any pertinent data, and the phone number and extension you will be calling.

6. Keep idle chit-chat under control. Purely social conversation is important to building good business and social relationships. It's good for morale and it also helps relax the tension. But it can be easily overdone. A twenty-minute fish story is probably eighteen minutes of waste.

7. Let the post office run your errands. The mail service can do endless things for you. A letter, if there is time, can often obtain the information for which you might have thought a trip necessary. Like the telephone, why "leg it" when all you need do is write a letter? The mails will also do such other things for you as shop and pay bills.

8. Make use of all spare time. Many businessmen handle the routine jobs during their spare moments. If a scheduled caller fails to appear, don't sit idly, tapping a pencil or biting your nails while you wait for

your next appointment to show up. Pick up another job and start on it.

Spend any short unexpected time you have signing mail or reading correspondence or reports. The time waiting to see a customer or prospect can be spent going over material in your briefcase. If you commute to work by train or bus, look through papers or business magazines, or spend your trip thinking. You might also take one or two nights a week at home reading business or other publications.

9. Keep the work in front of you, the distractions away. This is especially true if the task is one that is not particularly exciting. Put those other projects that might be more appealing away and concentrate only on the one job that must be completed.

10. Don't become bogged down in details. You should delegate and let somebody else worth considerably less per hour do the detail work. This calls for the selection of the employee who can be of the most assistance.

11. Get the important and hard jobs done first. Give the key matters your attention while you are at your peak. Save those "let-down" periods for opening and reading routine correspondence or some similar job. Start the tough jobs first thing in the morning.

12. Look for short cuts. Here, again, is the place to use an assistant if you have one. It is also wise to experiment. You might find a new time-saving approach.

13. Good working conditions are important. You'll do more and at a faster pace if your surroundings are as comfortable as possible. In general, a temperature

of 68-70 degrees, with humidity at 50 per cent, is best. Proper lighting is another factor that will ease your work.

14. Take a break from the tough ones. If a job has you stymied for the moment, back off and come back primed with new solutions.

15. Stop daydreaming. Don't build up a storehouse of ideas you'll "get around" to doing someday. If an idea is really good, it deserves to be put into action now.

Each of us is allotted only twenty-four hours a day. The time we waste is our own. If we make intelligent use of our time, we can be assured of the satisfaction that comes from the success we achieve in our work, and from the added hours we can begin to spend with our loved ones.

3

Don't Ever Stop Learning

Remember that old notion, "You can't teach an old dog new tricks?" Well, it's just not so.

No matter what your age, you can continue to increase your store of knowledge. This is an extremely important ability today because learning does go hand-in-hand with success. No one need stay in one job because he feels he lacks the capacity to grow. This chapter will show you how you can keep learning in a businesslike manner.

Take a New Look

The first step is to rid yourself of the idea that once you have finished formal schooling, whether at high school or college, your learning is ended except for improving your immediate job skills.

Nothing could be further from the truth. Educators tell us that one of the most desirable times to learn is the period between twenty and forty. But you needn't stop at the forty mark. If you have the desire to learn and if your learning skills have been kept in reasonably good working order, there is no reason why you shouldn't be able to learn well beyond the age of forty.

There are three simple guideposts to learning:

1. You must want to learn.
2. You must set goals for yourself.
3. You must use every possible technique of learning.

You Had the Desire to Learn

Remember when you were a youngster. Chances are, if you were a boy, you knew the batting average of every member of your favorite baseball team and those of every other leading star. You could probably name the starting lineups for every major league nine.

It was easy to remember these names and numbers because you wanted to. This is the important secret for learning. By pinpointing your reasons for wanting to master whatever knowledge you need, you've given yourself the desire to forge ahead. For example, knowledge of accounting, business law, salesmanship, or some technical skills will help you do a better job. This can lead to promotion, salary increases, and to a better life for your family. If you are in business for yourself, the ability to do a better job will assure the success of your enterprise, bringing with it all the rewards you desire.

Setting Your Goals

To learn anything effectively, you must first define your goals. Now sit back and study yourself to see if What can I do to help myself reach my goals?

Ask yourself some questions: What is my goal? What do I feel I must be able to do to reach this goal? Why must I reach this goal? What does reaching my target require in personality factors and in habits? What can I do to help myself reach my goals?

Every target must be a realistic one. Unless it is, you will face unbearable frustration. You can learn accounting. You can learn to play golf. You can learn to operate a piece of machinery. But don't forget: You can learn to swim, but it is certainly unrealistic to feel that you can swim an ocean, no matter how much you may want to.

Set your goals realistically, looking at both the positive and negative aspects of what you want to learn.

It is important to have confidence in your ability to learn. In your lifetime you've already acquired a tremendous amount of knowledge. The so-called simple skills such as walking, running, and talking were not easy for an infant. Today, you do arithmetic without a second thought, though your checkbook may sometimes not balance. But do you remember all those days from first grade on through high school, and even college, when you never thought you'd be able to understand how to add, subtract, multiply, divide, work with fractions, or be able to do advanced mathematics?

First, Learn How to Learn

Perhaps the first real step to learning anything is to learn *how* to learn. Educators have said the prime rule for learning is to learn something the correct way the first time. If you don't, you are then faced with triple the work. You've learned it. Then you must unlearn it. And then you must relearn the correct information. Doing it this way is a tremendous waste of time.

There are several so-called techniques for learning that will come in handy. For example, remember your first session with a lengthy poem in grade school? In my fifth grade it was Longfellow's poem "Barbara Fritchie." Believe it or not, I can still recite about half of the stanzas of that poem. We learned it by memorization and repetition. Memorization has its place in learning for adults, too, but remember that repetition can result in forgetting if the repetition becomes deadly dull.

One way to absorb information more easily is to understand what you are trying to learn. Information that is understood is retained much longer than knowledge that is merely memorized. Don't consider anything really learned until you fully understand it and can use it in its proper context in your work, or social life.

Similarly, practice in a routine task can make it appear that a person is highly skilled in his job. Too often a man with twenty years on his job has just re-learned it for the twentieth time over. He will probably never take the effort to try to improve his work.

Where Can You Learn?

The best way to improve and to increase your knowledge is to analyze what methods you need to reach your goals. Then make every effort to acquire these skills. In some industries, associations run technical, sales, and management training programs. In addition, the American Management Association, the American Marketing Association, the Sales Executive Clubs, and many other national groups provide courses that cut across industry lines.

The Federal Government, through such organizations as the Federal Business Development Bank, and various local governments also provide a variety of courses. Locally, many high schools have adult education classes that may provide the skills you require. Many universities and colleges and specialty schools provide both seminars and extension courses for adults. You can go for a degree, or attend one or two nights a week just for self-improvement.

This tremendous variety of courses will provide you with a wide range of information. You can learn about the latest techniques needed for your own job, or you can learn how to speed up your reading, improve your writing, step up your learning efficiency, or develop your memory. Later chapters in this book will provide you with background information and techniques for improving your ability in some of these personal areas.

Treasure House at Your Fingertips

Books can be real treasure houses of knowledge for you in your efforts to gain knowledge. Currently, many hardcover and paperback editions are available to the businessman-student. You might say these are your personal consultants. For a few dollars, or in some cases dimes, you can put the knowledge of the experts at your fingertips. None but the very largest business organizations can afford to hire all the consultants they need. You can acquire the knowledge of any expert for the simple price of a book.

Many publishers now make available a wide variety of self-improvement, management, sales, and technical books. The publisher of this book offers, in a series of books on aspects of business, many books that will help both the experienced businessman and those on the way up.

Motivating Yourself

Another secret of learning is to be highly motivated—to want deeply to acquire certain knowledge. You may feel it would be nice to be president of your company or to be the biggest independent businessman in town. But there is a difference between thinking how nice it would be and actually being motivated to become it.

More than likely, most of us tend to remember a fact or bit of information only as long as we think it necessary to do so. One college professor told a group of businessmen attending a seminar certain information. He divided his class into three groups. One section was told it would need the information for three days; another for a week. The third group understood they would need the information indefinitely. Follow-up testing showed that in 95 per cent of the cases the people retained the information only as long as they were told they would need it. They then promptly forgot it.

This case does show that once motivation is removed, a person tends to forget what he's learned. From a practical standpoint, then, the businessman-student should do a thorough job of selling himself on the rewards that will come to him if he learns and retains knowledge. If the desire for these rewards is strong enough, you can gain the necessary motivation to learn what is necessary for your advancement.

Getting More out of Reading

If your learning requires that you do a great deal of reading, here are some tips to help you absorb what you have read:

1. Relate what you read to your own experiences. Slower, more accurate learning is often faster than a speedy effort. You would be wise to think of specific examples that will relate to your studies as you read, rather than just rush to complete each chapter.

2. Take a break when you feel the need for one. This often gives the information time to sink in.

3. Provide yourself with periods of relaxation after attempting some very "heavy" learning. The more complete your relaxation the better, since upsets may cause you to fail to retain your new-found knowledge.

4. Stop studying when you get tired. Learning slows down when fatigue steps in.

5. Use every possible aid to help you absorb information. If possible turn off the phone. If you are working at a desk, see that it is neither too low or too high so that your body must assume an uncomfortable position. Don't use a chair that is too soft, because learning is something we usually consider a chore, and we may begin to doze off if the chair is too comfortable. Have a good reading light properly placed over your shoulder or over the desk and focused right on the paper. Remember, too, that a temperature of

68–70 degrees with humidity at 50 per cent is best for you to stay alert.

Your pencil or pen can also be a very valuable study aid. As you read, underline what you think important. Underlining offers you two major rewards. First, you are compelled to stay mentally alert so that you are more apt to find the important. Second, underlining helps you review. The underlined high spots are quickly spotted and redigested.

The best ways to use your pencil or pen for underlining are:

1. Underline topic sentences, key words, and phrases as you read.
2. If you find a series of sentences or paragraphs you want to remember, draw a vertical line to the right or left of this material.
3. If questions or thoughts are raised in your mind by the text, note them in the margins. These notations will serve as a reminder or memory-jogger when you reread the material.

Brief It Down

One of my friends, a graduate lawyer, has a technique which I've found extremely valuable for assimilating information. His legal firm assigned him to patent-law work, and he was asked to return to school for one year to pick up some engineering background. He found his return to the books difficult until he remembered his legal training. He began to write briefs for each lesson. These were actually summaries that proved to be his key study tool before an exam. He'd try to limit each brief of a chapter to about one or two hundred words. This mental exercise helped him better understand what he had read.

A businesspaper editor friend prides himself on reading a piece and then briefing it down to a lead paragraph, as if each article was a news story for his readers. What he was actually doing was *practicing* by pretending he was teaching his readers what he, himself, had learned.

Retaining What You Have Learned

We've already mentioned the importance of motivating yourself to retain what you have learned. There are other things that will help you keep this hard-earned information. Once you've learned something, use it as soon and as often as possible because practice does help you become more perfect. And try to use accurately what you've learned.

Try also to relate your new knowledge to your existing store of information. Not only will you bolster your past experience with new facts, but making continued use of new knowledge sets it more firmly in your mind. Another tip: you should begin to build source files about your job and interests. Clip magazine and newspaper articles. Either purchase books about your field or develop a bibliography of these titles for quick reference. This collection of facts can be one of your most valued possessions.

With these guidelines, you have the basis for continuing to absorb new knowledge in an effective manner for as long as you live. As you use this information in your everyday work, you will find that your knowledge, like fine silver, will improve with use.

4

How to Be Boss of Your Deskwork

A man or woman reaching for success is like a rocket aimed into outer space. The rocket has to free itself of the pull of gravity. You or I have to escape from the clutches of the paperwork that ties us to our desks.

I've met men who've felt that keeping their desks piled high with work made them look important. In most cases, their associates and superiors were really not impressed—they felt the overcrowded desk was really a sign of disorganization.

Unfortunately, paperwork and details are a major part of today's business life. The only way we can beat this affliction is to find ways to reduce our deskwork.

How to Be Inefficient

A first step is to admit that we are not quite as effective in our work as we thought we were. The major culprits are those who:

1. Tend to make useless and extra work out of every job they face.
2. Insist on doing all the detail work that really could be passed on to an assistant or someone who is qualified to handle the task. Remember, one of management's first rules is that the lowest-paid person qualified should do the work.
3. Allow work to pile up to such a degree that they are unable to handle real emergencies when they occur.
4. Refuse to make decisions when they first need making. They keep shunting the papers from one pile to another, and every time they show up at the top of a pile, they waste more time refreshing their memories with the pertinent facts.

Organization Will End the Log Jam

We can conquer these weaknesses. We've already learned that we must be boss. We must manage ourselves. Beating the busy-desk bugaboo simply means learning how to organize our work, our day, and our desk.

The man who develops techniques for handling his incoming and outgoing paperwork will stay on top of his job. In recent years I've discussed the problem of the "paper flood" with executives from many different types of businesses. They had many suggestions for speeding paperwork. On the pages that follow in this chapter, I've gathered the best of these ideas to help you stay on top of your work.

Most important: Try to avoid as much work as possible. While it may sound odd for an executive to avoid work, it's really not, if you are simply dividing and managing your work according to a plan.

How do you divide up your work among others? Let your secretary handle details for you. Next, put your assistant to work handling all possible remaining tasks. Then take a good look at what is left for you and see if there is any more work you can shift to either your secretary or your assistant.

Let's take a moment to look at this matter of an assistant. Perhaps you don't rate one today. You will tomorrow. It's a wise step to develop a good assistant. Besides taking a big load off your shoulders, he can give you a real feeling of security. When it is time for a vacation or a business trip, you'll be able to go knowing that you've left a man or woman ready and able to take over for you. Then again, if promotion comes for you, you've trained a man to step into your place. In many companies, the measure of a man is his ability to develop others.

Stay Out of Their Hair

Once you've trained your assistant and your secretary to help you, quit trying to keep your "fingers in every pie." You build confidence in your people only by giving them a chance to act on their own. Once you've assigned work, it should only be brought to your attention if something seems amiss.

If your people do run into a problem, see that they bring suggestions along to the problem conference. In this way, you need only make a decision based on the facts they present. The added advantage here is that your people learn to think for themselves.

It's another good rule of management to not meddle with those jobs you've given to others. As we said before, the lowest-paid qualified man or woman should be assigned each job.

One further suggestion about your relations with your assistants. Get out of the habit of calling too many conferences. In most cases, all these meetings do is take your people and you away from your work. Too many meetings may also tend to keep your people from making decisions on their own. They'll just sit and wait to hear your opinion, then echo it.

One of my former bosses, a vice president of a major oil company, limited his staff meetings to one a month. He saw to it that every member of his department, from the office boy up to himself and including the secretaries, took turns running the meetings. Not only did they learn responsibility, they also learned to think on their feet. I could also see the interest of these people flame brightly in their work, because they felt they had helped develop the projects.

Letting Your Secretary Help You

Now let's take a few moments considering your secretary. You hired her to help you, so why not let her do so? Experts estimate that some bosses waste almost half the working time of a secretary by not giving her enough responsibility.

One of the first things to do is to let this young lady handle your appointment schedule. She should know who you will see and how much time to allow for each visitor. She should also be kept up-to-date on those people you want to talk to over the phone. She can use her own judgment on your other callers.

Another time-consuming job for your secretary to assume is the handling of your files. Don't waste your time looking for papers. Let your secretary file everything under her own system. Let her get the papers you need when you need them. Keep out of her files. And don't keep papers on your desk—file them. Otherwise, they have a peculiar penchant for disappearing just when you want them.

When the mail comes to your desk, an experienced secretary should have already separated it into two or three piles. For example, pile one would hold those papers which demand your immediate attention. Pile two would contain those letters which can be answered by your secretary after you've penciled a brief notation on the bottom of each letter. Pile three contains the mail which does not require your immediate action.

Plan your dictation for one certain time each day; either in the morning or afternoon. In this way, your secretary can plan her schedule to coincide with your demands for her time. This regular schedule also allows her to make the best use of her time. Most men told me they preferred to dictate to their secretaries in the morning, right after looking over the mail. This permitted their secretaries to transcribe the dictation and to ask any questions they may have for their bosses before the working day ends. The girl was then ready to start the next working day fresh, with a clean desk.

These men also felt firmly that dictation should be limited to once a day, except for emergencies. Irregular dictation schedules waste a secretary's time, they felt.

If you share a secretary with one or two others, arranging your schedule for once-a-day dictation is a great help to all concerned.

Another suggestion for helping your secretary in her work is to set aside a few minutes each day for you to talk over projects with her. This keeps her informed about your current business activities, and also keeps her from interrupting you with questions throughout the day.

Giving Her the Proper Tools

Give your secretary the tools to do her job quickly, accurately, and easily. A good electric typewriter can shorten typing time and also be less tiring. A comfortable chair and desk will also help improve her efficiency.

There is a great variety of dictating equipment available. Such equipment has the advantage of permitting you to dictate whenever and wherever you wish. This is especially true with the small portable units now available. You can dictate at home, in the car, in your office, or anywhere and just turn the record, tape, belt, or cylinder over to your secretary or the typing pool.

One last point about your secretary. Many executives I know place their travel and meeting schedules in the hands of these capable women. A woman seems to have a knack for arranging a trip, planning a luncheon, or setting up a meeting. Get these time-consuming jobs out of your own hands.

A More Efficient You

Now let's get back to the work pile you've left for yourself. First of all, learn how to read faster.

We'll devote our next chapter to that, but now let's get down to the specifics of self-management to help you control your desk work.

Earlier we talked about the importance of managing yourself. This ability is never in greater demand than when you must handle miscellaneous deskwork. I've put together some rules for managing detail that I have picked up in my travels. Really, they are very simple.

Analyze every job that comes to you and schedule it for a definite time. Too many men and women run around, working at a lot of different jobs at one time and completing none. When you start on a task, finish it. Don't put off making a decision about it. This only means that you must again review the whole problem later and still come up with a solution. It's double or triple work for you.

Many men handle the many easy, short-time projects first. They say this helps them warm up. They can then complete the fewer but larger jobs without having the threat of many small tasks hanging over them.

For the big jobs, the best way is to start on the unpleasant ones first, while you are feeling fresh. However, if one project becomes too tough, put it aside for the time being. You can return to it when you are fresher. You'll find that after taking a break you may return to the task with a fresh approach.

One of the best rules is to keep work right in front of you, to haunt you. I think this is the actual philosophy behind these fancy modern desks of ours. In the old roll-top affairs, work was easily pigeonholed out of sight. In contrast, the modern desk is only a work space sitting on either legs or a filing cabinet. Leave the work right on top of the desk. Most of us are orderly enough to be a bit ashamed of others seeing our messy desk. If the work sits out in plain sight, we'll try our best to complete the project.

Look for the Short Cuts

Use whatever short cuts you can find. One of my friends simply returns any letters that do not require filing with his answer written across the bottom. If the letter must be retained, his secretary prepares a letter based on his notations for his signature.

Another handy time-saver is the telephone. You can use it for any matter that does not require documentation. This method is certainly much faster than the mails.

Keep in constant touch with those people who work with you. Such communication will prevent misunderstandings and avoid lost time.

Another suggestion: Keep your door shut. Most executives have learned that it does not pay to keep their office doors wide open to everybody. Too many well-meaning callers are actually time-wasters. You can kill valuable hours every day just talking about sports, fishing, or exchanging the latest jokes. Perhaps you'll be called antisocial, but if you are the least bit capable in your normal relations with your associates, you'll quickly kill this reputation. The quality and quantity of your work will show that you are a man to be counted upon.

As you grow in stature and responsibility, you'll find more and more requests come to you from outside your own business. You'll be asked to serve on committees, to make speeches, to join business and civic groups. This is a sign of recognition. Each of these activities, however, requires some of your valuable time and energy.

Some community or business association work is necessary as your contribution to a stronger local and national community and to the growth of your own industry. It is a good rule, however, to be very selective before you accept any invitation. Pick and choose those activities which can accomplish the most for your own family, or community, or industry, as well as your business.

And as one last suggestion: Watch the briefcase. Too many men get in the habit of carrying their case back and forth to work every night. After a while they lose interest in a constant chain of night work and just go through the motions of packing the case every evening.

If you must take work home, try to do so on just a few nights each week. Each of us must develop a full, well-rounded way of life. This will bring with it peace of mind, greater health, and the vigor to work at keeping your desk cleared and yourself ready for important action.

5

Read Faster to Read Better

Take a close look at your watch as you begin to read the following typical business magazine article:

> The farm—one of the LP-Gas industry's best customers, present and potential—is to play a major role in the America of the future. An America that's to be a vastly bigger place with more people, more workers, and bigger markets.
>
> All these things and more, too, are projected for the year 1975 by the closest thing we yet have to a time traveling machine—the Resources for Freedom Report. Predictions contained in this report are those of a group of experts brought together to study U.S. resources in the light of future demands.
>
> The massive five-volume report which marks the efforts of the President's Policy

Commission contains material gathered from Government and private industry's sources. Heading the commission was William S. Paley, Columbia Broadcasting System's chairman of the board.

In a nutshell, here is the United States of 1975. This country will have about 193,400,000 people; cities will have about 50 per cent more dwellings; employment will be close to 80,000,000; passenger vehicles will number 65,000,000; trucks about 20,000,000; and the standard of living is to be at a peak hard to visualize.

A big job in the growing years ahead is to fall to the farmer. Land is the essential base for the production of most of the needed resources—both food and nonfood. Increasing population and better standards of living in the next quarter of a century coupled with greater industrial requirements for agricultural raw materials will impose a heavy burden on the farmer and his land.

The farms of the United States must supply many raw materials important to industry—cotton, wool and other fibres, hides and skins, fats and oils for paints and soaps, tobacco, industrial alcohol and countless others. In addition, a number of crops grown primarily for food or feed have secondary uses as sources of industrial materials as plastics and starch.

The Materials Policy Commission found

itself confronted by two great questions in analyzing the agricultural question: (1) Can the farmland of the United States provide the food and industrial materials needed in 1975? and (2) Is any change to take place in the relation of agriculture to the nation's economy?

In answer to the first, the commission predicts that agriculture can meet the needs of the U.S. of the future. To the second, the commission says no. It feels that basically, meeting estimated requirements will be a domestic responsibility just as it is today.

Now, let's delve deeper into the problem facing the farmer. The U.S. of 1975 will be a highly urbanized nation. This means that the present trend of increasing demand for farm products and a declining farm labor force will continue. Between 1939 and 1949, the number of persons employed in agriculture dropped nearly 10 per cent to 10,756,000. In 1950 alone, 400,000 left the farms. In 1975, only an estimated 7,000,000 will remain part of the farm labor team.

That means less labor will have to fill the needs of 28 per cent more people. The 1975 population of 193,400,000 will require 41 per cent more food and will consume 25 per cent more farm nonfoods—a boost of 38 per cent for all farm products. New industrial uses for farm products, not counted in all estimates, might raise this to 40 per cent.

To handle the enormous task set before them with the smaller labor force available, farmers must continue the trend to complete mechanization. The commission estimates that needed production will require more than a 40 per cent production increase from each farm worker. This can only be accomplished by a highly mechanized force using the latest technological methods.

The needs of agriculture for machinery and equipment over the next 25 years are to be in the main for replacements, the commission feels. New types of machines will be used for replacements. In addition, agriculture will continue to substitute machines for hand labor. This means an increasing use of mechanical cotton pickers, field hay bailers and field hay choppers and other harvesting machines, and also new types of tillage equipment to replace hoeing, chopping, and the like. (Reprinted with permission from *LP-Gas* Magazine.)

You've just read seven hundred words. Discounting the fact that the estimates may be a bit outdated and that your business might not be in the least bit concerned with agriculture, this is the type of reading the business men and women must do, all the time. If you have what is considered good speed-reading ability, it should have taken you just about one minute to read this excerpt. If you failed to come closer than three minutes, you are probably lost in a paperwork jungle.

This might sound a bit extreme, but it is true. One look at your everyday mail and the extra-company correspondence which pours over your desk will point out this job requirement. You must be able to read fast if you are to do the required work.

Reading, Just Reading

At a meeting of the American Management Association some time ago, conferees said that executives spent between 25 and 75 per cent of their time just reading. This work load consisted of reading memos and reports, general correspondence, business and trade publications, product bulletins, advertising materials, and other assorted printed matter.

It was also reported that employees at other levels spent up to two hours of every day in reading.

Since the average reader crawls along reading about 200 to 250 words per minute, it stands to reason that the best investment you can make is to improve your reading ability. Say you can boost it from this low mark of 250 words per minute up to 500. You have cut your reading time in half. If you can raise it to about 700 (the figure the experts consider necessary for an adult) you might be able to read everything you need to in only about 40 per cent of the time you now spend. Since every minute you save is worth money to your career, it really pays to learn how you can convert reading time to dollars.

Read as an Adult

We actually have only two major defenses against the paper flood. We can throw as much as possible into the wastebasket, or we can learn to read as an adult should.

Yes, I said as an adult! Too many of us have a set of reading skills that are stagnated at the level of a sixth-grade student. It's not really our fault. We were taught to read by methods that are inadequate to meet the demands of the modern business world.

Like many skills that we fail to develop to the fullest, we stopped learning to read at a young age. Some of us actually begin to regress, and our reading ability is simply an understanding of the meaning of the common words and the habit of reading from left to right.

Luckily, reading skills can be improved at any age. You can advance from a mediocre 250 words per minute to 700 or even 1,000 or more words per minute. With this greater ability will come improved understanding and self-growth.

Slowpokes Don't Really Understand More

One of the great fallacies is the belief that a slow reader understands and remembers more. It's just not so. Reading specialists have found that the faster you can move down a page, the more you will have the opportunity to comprehend. This has been proven time and time again by tests of college students. They prove that a good reader picks out the essential ideas and puts together the "big picture."

Like most rules, there is an exception. We must understand that certain types of material naturally slow us down. This often may be the result of our own interest level, and why most of us will race through fiction and seemingly crawl through a company report.

Your Mind—The Key to Good Reading Habits

The basic idea in the more modern reading schools is that your mind controls the act of reading. A slow reader may make ten or even twenty eye movements for each printed line. A faster reader will comprehend the same line in only two or three eye movements. The secret, therefore, is to make your mind read efficiently.

The good reader attacks a printed page as if he were eating in a restaurant. The menu, his instructions to the waiter, and the arrival of the food tell him how to go about the act of eating. In like manner, the good reader quickly checks the title, chapter, subheadings, picture captions if there are any, and the first paragraph to see if he must read the piece before him.

This investigation also tells you how fast you'll have to read and how much you can expect to get out of the material.

Like the diner as he eats, you must also have a strong sense of purpose before reading anything. You must know what you are reading, why you are reading it, and how much you will profit by reading it.

How to Pick Up Speed

Let's list some rules or guides for faster reading. These will be expanded later in this chapter.

1. *Preview your material.* Check titles, subheads, captions, first paragraph to determine if the material is worth reading and what reading speed is required.

2. *Don't look back.* Once you've started, keep moving on. Avoid the temptation to go back and look again at some of the ideas you may feel you don't fully understand. You can come back to review later, after the entire piece is finished.

3. *Find the main ideas.* Discover the one idea in each paragraph that is important. Also note the directional signals such as: "also," "such as," "but," "yet," "etc."

4. *Memorize.* As you read, select the facts that are important to you. Store them away in your brain and memorize them for future use.

Now, let's put these rules to work at helping us read faster and to get more out of what we are reading.

Reading by Thought Units

You can gain speed by simply reading in longer thought units. This is a matter of recognizing entire groups of words instead of picking up each word, one at a time. This is more easily done than it would seem, because the writers put sentences together with key words and phrases. The other words and phrases are actually just subsidiaries to the main thought.

If you will follow the key words, moving your eyes from one sense group to the next, you will soon find yourself pausing only two or three times a line. The slower reader is constantly running into road blocks and detours as he hops from one word to the next, making ten or twenty or more hops before he finishes a line.

Earlier we said the good reader analyzes what he will read before he actually starts. He is usually flexible and is able to slip from one speed to another, based on the requirements of the material after he has previewed it. He also quickly makes the decision to try to master all the facts or to merely look for essential ideas.

Working with the Author

Once the preview is complete, you dive in and begin communicating with the author. Don't fight the writer. If he is the least bit good, he has placed his idea on a word pedestal so that you can quickly find it. This is usually true because the average well-written English sentence contains only one important idea.

Your reading will speed up as you learn to ignore such things as transitions, connections, and modifiers. When you've done this, all you have left are the main subject and verb. Then you isolate the main idea and subsidiary thoughts. You have a clear understanding of what the writer meant, and you can move right on to the next paragraph.

Your reading movement is assisted by the so-called directional words that move you along from one important idea to the next. These are words the author has put there to help you. Your mind should only glance at them, and move right on to isolate the major thought. The "directional words" are then forgotten.

Such "directional words" include: "and," "also," "likewise," "such as," "furthermore," "in addition to." These words simply tell you that the author will introduce no new ideas or changes in thought. The track ahead is cleared for you to read on at top speed.

There are other connecting words, however, which are designed to flag your attention. They tell you to look out for a change. These words include: "but," "yet," "otherwise," "although," "on the other hand."

Mining the Gold

The skilled reader is like a locomotive. He keeps on a straight track. He is not interested in the words themselves, only in what the writer is trying to tell him. Again it is a matter of seeking out the main points and ideas of the author. You don't let the details bog you down. When you've finished each piece, you understand just what the author meant even if you don't remember the exact words he used to get his idea across.

Remembering details and facts requires that you pick out what you want to retain. You then mentally organize these prized facts and store them away in a corner of your brain for future use.

Skimming for Greater Speed

Many of the fastest readers have the ability to skim. They use a wide glance of their eyes to preview upcoming facts. These skimmers recognize key words and ideas. They have trained themselves to understand a writer's attempts at organization.

Skimmers of the slow variety read by the lines. Their faster compatriots draw a mental line down the center of the page. They read only the words on either side of the line, and miss very little of importance.

What actually happens is two things. First, the skimmer's eyes are picking up and interpreting the words alongside the words they actually read through what is called peripheral vision. Peripheral vision is the reason for the success of many athletes and good drivers. You can practice to achieve such a wide glance.

Second, the reader has his own sense of organization. His knowledge of the language and subject is such that he is able to infer the total meaning from the facts the author has placed on either side of the invisible line. Skimming is a most valuable technique, but it takes long practice to master this art.

Practice Makes Perfect

Once you are able to read more, you will find that you are able as well to keep up with the latest ideas in your field. This ability can mean promotion if you work for others. If you have your own business, it can mean increased prosperity because you've learned new ideas and techniques.

Once you have reached what you consider good reading speed, keep the ability at peak performance. You can do this only by regular and constant practice. No matter what you pick up to read, peruse it at your top speed for facts and ideas. The literature can be fiction, light nonfiction, a technical report, or a memo from the boss.

We've spent this chapter describing how a person can increase his speed and understanding through faster, more accurate reading. If you want, you can do it yourself by constantly trying to step up your speed. In addition, there are speed reading courses available from specialized speed reading schools and through many of the nation's colleges.

Many men and women have practiced by simply setting an alarm clock and then timing themselves to see how many words they read. They continually try to improve on their past performance. Others do it a bit more scientifically—they tally up the seconds it takes them to complete an article or chapter, or report, divide this figure into the total number of words, then multiply by sixty to convert their total words per minute.

No matter what method you use to step up your reading speed, the payoff can mean more efficiency. With this efficiency will come greater success for you.

6

Stay Healthy to Accomplish More

To manage your own business or to do the job for another person at the fullest efficiency, your body must be able to meet all demands forced upon it. If you are tired all the time, if you find it difficult to meet constant pressures, you are operating under a severe handicap. It could destroy your business or your career.

To be physically fit is to be in good health. Unfortunately, we seldom think of the state of our health until illness strikes. Then it is often too late to do anything about it. You know your business or job, inside and out. You keep up with the latest techniques and tools. You look for short cuts. Why else would you be reading this book? Yet, how many of you have ever taken the trouble to find out how to keep this marvelous machine we call the body working at full strength?

A few health hints kept in mind while you are well will help *keep* you fit. Here are a few suggestions for you.

Proper Fuel Is Required

The fuel for our body is the food we eat. Americans pride themselves on an abundance of nourishing and tastily prepared foods of endless variety. And rightly we should. Today, children grow taller, stronger, and healthier than our ancestors did largely because of better and more plentiful food, rich in minerals and vitamins.

With all these advantages on our side, many of us, through poor habits, eat improperly. Some of us eat foods high in caloric value and low in vitamins and other essential food nutrients. These are so-called empty calories. If their intake is continued over a long period of time, they often result in an overweight person with relatively poor resistance to illness.

Others eat excessive amounts of fat, especially those of the saturated type found in animal fat, butter, and cheese. A diet that is excessively high in such fats may predispose a person to early arteriosclerosis and coronary heart disease.

The food we eat provides not only fuel for warmth and energy, it also regulates many of our body functions. Improper diet may reduce your resistance to disease, may impair vision, may cause skin disturbances and other common ailments.

What Is a Good Diet?

What is a good diet? It is one that is moderate in the number of calories, balanced in the proportions of various food substances, rich in vitamins and minerals, and relatively low in fat, especially those of the saturated variety.

It is wise to remember just a few rules about the makeup of the food that fuels our body. Proteins are said to be the building blocks of the body. They help our bodies repair damaged tissues, develop muscles, and provide other necessary body fluids. Proteins are found in meats, fish, fowl, and cheeses.

Carbohydrates supply the quick energy we need. They are found in sugars and starches. Fats are also required to give us needed energy and to develop the heat our body requires.

A good diet implies that food will be eaten regularly at regular times. Your diet should be varied and diversified. You should allow yourself sufficient time for a leisurely meal. This is most important in combating the buildup of tensions, as we will see in Chapter 7. Overeating at any one meal should be avoided.

Most of us will, by choice, select a diet of good variety. However, if you find yourself overweight or underweight, or just not feeling up to par, it would be wise to consult your physician and include in the discussion a study of your dietary habits.

Exercise Is Important

A certain amount of exercise is required if we are to stay physically fit. It is not necessary for you to go into heavy training as an athlete would, but a proper amount of exercise compatible with your age and body is of definite benefit.

Aside from keeping your muscles and body in shape, exercise will help relax mental tensions and ease a tired mind. A feeling of well-being that follows a period of exercise will help you over the periods of lassitude and fatigue that frequently follow a trying day's work.

Your exercise should be regularly scheduled and it should be geared to your own physical characteristics. Here, your physician should be consulted so he can suggest the best exercises for you. For those in the older age groups, simple calisthenics or sitting-up exercises are adequate and beneficial. For the more agile, swimming, handball, tennis, or golf may be more appropriate.

Luckily, we can exercise frequently and without too much preparation. For example:

1. Walk whenever and wherever you can. If you must take a bus to the office, get off six or eight blocks early. The tempo of your walking will awaken your mind and set you up, ready for work. Take a walk after lunch. Some experts recommend that we spend at least one hour walking every day.

2. Work around your home. Push the lawn mower and other garden tools with vigor. When you have to move a chair, pick it up and carry it—don't just push it.

3. Climbing stairs every day gives your knees a chance to bend and your legs a chance to lift your body.

4. Use every possible opportunity to exercise. Don't sit down to pull on your socks and shoes. Stand up and reach over to get them on. These bends every morning do help you stay in shape. When you shower or bathe, stoop and bend your body as you wash and then dry yourself.

Adequate Rest Is Essential

Equally important as exercise is proper rest and sleep. Sleep is vitally necessary to help you recover from mental and physical fatigue. Without sufficient and proper sleep, you can quickly become irritable, restless, and inefficient.

Many of us fail to get enough sleep simply because we can't afford to spend the full eight hours necessary each night. Others may be unable to sleep enough for a variety of reasons; such insomnia may be due to physical illness, emotional strain, worry, or excessive amounts of coffee or other stimulants.

You can help yourself to more relaxed sleep by setting up conditions that are conducive to good sleeping. See that the room temperature and humidity are comfortable. Choose a mattress that is just right for your back. If you have eaten heavily, walk around the block before you climb into bed.

Try to forget your business or your job or other worries. One way to do this is to relax in bed with an interesting book. Another way is to take a relaxing shower or a warm bath.

Some of us worry so much about not being able to fall asleep that we get tense and just can't sleep. Try to stop worrying about falling asleep. Once your head hits the pillow, just relax. Sleep will come.

If you are troubled with insomnia, act fast to find out what is wrong because it can undermine your health. If you cannot correct the insomnia by simple means, your physician should be promptly consulted.

Your Eyes and Ears

Of our five senses, seeing and hearing are probably the most important. Safeguarding your sight and hearing should be foremost in your mind when you consider your physical fitness.

The eye is made up of many kinds of very specialized tissues controlled by muscles and nerves. It is protected by a layer of cushioning fat set in a bony framework which protects all but the exposed portion of your eye. Your eye is virtually a miniature camera, complete with lens and the iris as the diaphragm.

Although your eyes are placed in a position that provides them with a good deal of protection, they are still subject to many types of injury. These include damage by dust, fumes, chemicals, and excessive ultraviolet radiation which may be encountered in sunlight or from a welder's arc. If you should be exposed to such hazards, it is important to remember to wear protective glasses or goggles. Many types have been designed to meet the different occupational dangers.

Aside from injuries, your eyes are subject to a number of ills. Many persons are born with eyes with lenses which have slight defects in their contour or shape. To enable their eyes to function properly, it is necessary to correct the defect with glasses. Children who do poorly in school are often those who are handicapped by faulty vision and require eyeglasses.

Current living and business practice demands more and more use of your eyes, and it is very important to have them checked periodically. Television has added another heavy burden to our already overworked eyes.

In later years the eyes may be subject to such diseases as glaucoma and cataracts. If they are detected early, much can be done to delay the progress of these disabling infirmities. A competent ophthalmologist with his special equipment can quickly ascertain whether or not signs of these diseases are developing.

Take Care of Your Hearing

Some people feel that hearing is even more important than sight. Hearing failures often manifest themselves in the middle years of life. They can be caused by a variety of things. Some hearing problems come simply from an accumulation of wax in the ear canals. This accumulation can be easily removed by a physician. Other hearing problems are caused by the scarring and immobilization of the tiny bones which conduct sounds in the middle ear. Such deafness can often be helped by surgery.

Other types of deafness are caused by degeneration of the nerves which conduct the sound impulses from the ear to the brain. Such types of deafness can be helped by having fitted a proper type of hearing aid.

Infections are frequent in ears. Earaches or running ears should send you promptly to a physician for treatment so any permanent ear damage may be avoided. You should report any signs of diminishing hearing to your physician so he can determine the cause and begin proper treatment without delay.

Don't Forget Those Physical Checkups

The importance of periodic checkups by your physician cannot be overstressed. Most of us consult a doctor only if we are seriously ill or have have some serious injury or accident. Some of us take the trouble to see our physician for more minor ills. Very few of us actually see our physician for a general physical examination every year.

Periodic examinations have many important advantages. Aside from picking up illnesses or diseases in their early stages when they are more amenable to treatment, annual examinations permit your physician to know you and your body when you are well. He will therefore be better able to treat you more effectively when you are ill. He can guide you and help you to stay well.

You will find that medical checkups vary in scope, but they usually include the following procedures:

1. A general examination includes listening to your heart and lungs with a stethescope. Most abnormalities in these two organs can generally be discovered by a thorough general physical examination.

2. A chest X-ray is important to discover if you have such diseases of the lungs as tuberculosis, and to indicate whether the outline of the heart and large blood vessels is normal.

3. A blood pressure determination is a simple, painless measurement, performed by wrapping an inflatable bag, connected to a meter, around your arm. From the blood pressure measurement, your physician will gain important information as to the state of your circulation and general health.

4. A urinalysis is of great value in detecting diseases of the kidneys, as well as other unrelated diseases such as diabetes.

Putting together the results of the examination, laboratory tests, and such information as you bring him regarding the way you feel, your doctor gains a good picture of the state of your health.

He may make some recommendations, such as taking off excess weight. He may prescribe some treatment for a disorder that he has discovered. Or he may find everything in good order. If this latter is the case, you have reason to leave his office with the feeling of elation and well-being that comes from the knowledge that you are physically fit and capable of meeting every test thrown at you.

7

Taking the Tension Out of Your Job

Are you spending ten, twelve, or fourteen hours a day on your job? Chances are that some of this time is wasted, and that this waste is brought on by tension. Luckily, there are ways to overcome the mental or nervous strains that cause tension to build up.

First of all, let's see just where these tensions and pressures come from. Tension is not a new disease which affects us when we become adults. Most of us have lived with these pressures since birth. At first there were the unconscious pressures to learn to walk and talk. As we grew older, we met the pressures of tests in school, of making the team or club, of getting a date or getting married, or finding a job or starting your own business.

Today, we face almost constant pressures. Most of us go through mental changes when we are stimulated by a problem or irritation of some sort. Tension can arise both on the job and in our social lives. Tension can develop because we are rushing to complete a job within a definite span of time. It may arise if we need to meet a dollar or item quota in selling . . . or face a load of bills, or even need money to get married or to send our children to college. As we are given added responsibility over work and people, we take on new pressures.

Part of the battle is simply to understand that your work will bring about tension, and that these pressures will often be the real cause of both a tired feeling and of a possible poor job or social performance.

The Animals Have It Easy

Our big problem is that a natural release from tension does not come easy. An irritated animal may strike out at its tormentors. What happens if a customer calls to "give you hell" for something that is not your fault? Or suppose the boss forgets a promised bonus. Right away you become angry—and you tense up. You'd like to punch your boss or the customer in the nose, but that is impossible. In fact, you can't let either know how irritated you are.

So you begin to steam under the collar. Soon the tension has backed up and you've got a headache, or a backache, maybe it's an upset stomach. You feel awful. Your work, what there is of it that you do finish, suffers. The rest piles up so that you start the next day with a load of today's work to face you.

How to Avoid the Tension Buildup

You can avoid all such tension and keep operating at top efficiency—if you act to keep tension from building up in the first place.

We know of two ways to overcome tension. The first is exercise—that activity that too many of us either forget or ignore. But exercise is not the full answer. Where it fails to provide complete relief, a program of self-management will often provide the solution.

Just where does tension seem to build up in you? For most of us the uncomfortableness seems to stay localized in our neck or shoulder muscles or down our back. Tension can be dispelled from these areas by a series of physical actions you can take to stop the buildup. A training director for a large corporation, speaking at a convention I attended some years ago, suggested the following exercises to men and women chained to their desks in a sedentary job. Here they are:

1. Stretch out your arms and take a deep breath every time you sit down.
2. Every ten or fifteen minutes, straighten up and then shrug your shoulders to relax yourself.
3. Lean back in your chair and have a good stretch every half-hour.
4. Don't keep your phone at your elbow. Set it

so that you have to stretch out to reach it and to put it back.

5. Lean over and touch your toes everytime you get ready to stand up.

These are five very simple exercises. Practice them until they become second nature to you. You'll be surprised how well they will help you keep tension at bay.

Try Desk "P.T."

It would be wonderful if everyone of us could or would spend an hour of every day exercising. Unfortunately, very few of us can find the time to do so. Even if we could, how many actually would?

Suppose you could shut the door of your office, or draw an invisible screen around you if you work out in a "bull pen." The first thing you should do would be a few quick pushups. Then you'd touch your toes five or ten times. If you did this, you would have toned yourself up for the whole day in just about five minutes' time.

The trouble is, who will do it? Some of us would be too embarrassed at what the boss or our coworkers or employees would say. Others of us are just too lazy.

These two exercises were out of the question for a magazine editor I once worked with. However, he resorted to what he called "Desk P.T." One of the best of his exercises is a sort of chair pushup. Try it as a quick tension reliever.

Place one hand on each arm of your chair. Push down until your arms have straightened out and you have raised your body out of the chair. Now let yourself down and raise yourself up and out of your chair again. Do five or ten of these two or three times a day.

Another of his office exercises was a so-called desk pushup. In this exercise you lean against your desk, with your hands touching the desk. Now use your hands to push yourself out and away from the desk until you are standing straight. Now back down and then out until you are again standing straight. Do ten of these at a time. The desk pushup is not strenuous, but it is a good toner-up. These are less work than a prone pushup from the floor, and they really seem to help dispel tension.

Avoid slumping in your chair. This puts an uncomfortable weight on the base of your spine. Assume a posture that will enable you to breathe properly.

The Atmosphere Is Important, Too

Try to avoid working in a stuffy room. If ventilation is poor, you'll have to make greater effort to complete your work. To function most efficiently, your brain cells must have plenty of fresh air.

Incidentally, you won't tire as fast if your office or place of work is kept at 67–70 degrees. If the temperature drops lower or climbs higher, your body needs more energy to operate at fullest efficiency. Tests have shown that at 90 degrees your body expends 50 per cent more energy than if the temperature is at 67–70 degrees.

Rest periods are as vital to a mental laborer as to a physical laborer. The type of relaxation required, however, can be completely different. The physical laborer needs complete relaxation. In contrast, the mental laborer should engage in a mildly stimulating activity to keep his alertness at the proper level.

You might play cards or chess, or read a book or a newspaper. Playing the dart board, that center of the English pub, is a perfect way to relax and to stretch cramped muscles.

Exercising Away from the Office

You should follow some sort of regular physical conditioning to keep your body toned up and the tension down. In our last chapter we discussed exercise and walking. Both are vitally important as aids in keeping your performance tip-top.

Actually, you can do much to keep yourself fit while you are commuting to your place of business. Use the stairs as much as possible. Walk to and from train or parking lot. At lunchtime, take a walk and enjoy the sights and the fresh air. One of the best ways to digest your food is to take a walk to admire the pretty girls. More often than not, you'll come back with your mind cleared and ready for an afternoon's business.

Let me advance another radical thought. Take your whole family for an after-dinner walk. You will all feel better for it and sleep will come that much faster than if you all had slumped down in front of your television set.

I have my own formula for relaxing at night, even if I had to break a rule and bring some important work home. As soon as I finish kissing the family, I take the dog for a walk—just short of a half-mile each way. Then I wash up and change clothes, and we all sit down for supper.

After supper, I relax with the kids until their bedtime. Then I do anything that needs doing—a do-it-yourself project that the wife has thought up, the rare office work, attend a civic meeting, or just plain relaxation. Before going to bed, I take the dog for his last walk of the night. Then a shower and I'm off to bed.

Incidentally, scientists at the University of California say the quickest and most effective way to banish physical tiredness is to climb under a cold shower. Perhaps it is a shock, but it does work.

Ask Your Doctor First

There is no doubt about it, engaging in a regular program of exercise of one kind or another will help you stay in shape and keep tension from developing. The only reason for not exercising is physical. Each person's case depends upon his own condition. The best thing to do is to go to your doctor and ask him to prescribe the best conditioning program for you. Let him be your guide for putting you in tip-top condition.

Self-Management Is Also Important

Now, let's get back to the other method for ending job pressures. It is simply the self-management techniques we are discussing in this book. One way to avoid strain and pressure is to have your job under your thumb.

With good self-management, you quickly isolate your problems and find out what causes them. Next you decide on the best way to solve these problems. The methods for self-management of your time and for cutting deskwork described in Chapters 1, 2, and 4 will do much to help you to a happier, healthier business life, and the resulting satisfactory home life.

8

How to Remember Names and Faces

One of the prime skills that lead to success in business is the ability to get along with people. A good first step in this direction is to be able to remember who they are. Everybody likes to be thought important. When you forget a person's name or face, you tell him that you didn't think him important enough to learn who he is.

After all, you wouldn't forget Mickey Mantle or Roger Maris once you had met them. You certainly wouldn't forget somebody like Jayne Mansfield. Remember, Joe Doe, Jean Smith, Tom Brown, or Salvatore Angelo are just as important—more important if they are customers or associates of one type or another.

Today, you can conquer this mental failing. Thousands of busy men and women are using certain tested principles to improve their memories, and they are finding that all it takes is the desire to remember plus some hard work.

Your Memory Can Be Improved

No matter how poor you feel your memory is, it can be made better. The experts tell us the memory is like a muscle. The more you exercise it, the more you strengthen it.

People have poor memories because they are too lazy to have good memories. Too many of us just barely observe what is going on in the world around us. Scientists say that most of us are going around using less than a quarter of our full brainpower. Quick now, can you remember the numbers on the license plates on your car?

How to Sharpen Your Memory

When you visit a customer or prospect at his business or his home, you find it easy to identify him because you expect to see him amid certain familiar surroundings. Even if you can't remember what he looks like, there is little chance that this failing will embarrass you when you arrive.

But there is every chance that you might meet this same person unexpectedly on the street, at a restaurant, or at a meeting. With your points of reference gone, you could have a very offensive memory blackout. It might even cost you business.

Perhaps the one embarrassing moment that started me on the road to memory improvement began with my wife and me in 1953. We were trying to get a plane back home from Miami Beach during the height of the tourist season. In desperation I called a friend who was vice president of one of the large liquefied petroleum gas companies in the area. He told me just to sit tight and he would get back to me. Less than a half-hour later we had our confirmed reservations.

Three months later I was sitting in the coffee shop of the Atlanta Biltmore Hotel with some other gas men who were attending a convention I was covering. A good-looking grey-haired man sitting across the room waved to me. I just couldn't place him, but I waved back anyway. After paying his check he walked by the table and said hello and asked about my wife. After small talk he left and I sat there hoping he hadn't noticed my confusion. Later I saw him across the lobby and asked the convention chairman his name. It was the man who had gone out of his way to arrange our plane transportation. Right then and there I vowed to do everything I could to strengthen that lazy memory of mine.

One of the first things to do is to sharpen your powers of observation. But remember one thing: unsystematic, helter-skelter efforts rarely pay off. You must start to fill your memory bank in a systematic manner.

Basically, the job is two-fold: You must recognize the person's face or appearance, *and* remember his name. Your eye is the key to recalling the face.

Remembering his name depends almost entirely on the sounds that reach your brain through your ears.

Take Daily Mental Exercises

Specialists in memory improvement say that the first step is to take daily mental exercises to stimulate your sluggish memory. Here's a typical exercise. Shut your eyes and see if you can visualize every detail of your office. Where is each article located? How many shelves are there in the bookcases? How many panes of glass in each window? How many trade magazines are piled on your desk? Which magazine is on top?

When you can recall all the details of your office, try other rooms that are less familiar.

Exercise two will help improve your powers of concentration. You can do this exercise at home tonight in your favorite chair. See if you can recall everything you did today. Whom did you talk to? About what? Where did you eat? What did you have for lunch? If you had a luncheon companion, what did he or she eat?

Another good test that will help make you the life of the party is to concentrate on the funny stories and jokes you hear during a meeting or a day's work. Sit down at night and see how many you can remember.

Recognizing Faces

Several days of these mental calisthenics and you are ready to concentrate on the really big task of remembering people. There are six major steps to remembering faces. Here they are:

1. Be interested enough to want to remember the people you meet. After my embarrassing moment with the friend who had been able to arrange my transportation back from Miami Beach, I decided it was well worth my while to try to remember every person I would meet with whom I might have possible future contacts.

2. Look at the face. Get a general impression of the features. Study hair, eyes, nose, the shape of the head and ears, and any other features or physical characteristics.

3. Find a special feature or characteristic to help you remember that person. For example: John L. Lewis' bushy eyebrows, Dwight Eisenhower's high forehead, Winston Churchill's bulldog look, Brigitte Bardot's pout and hairdo, Jackie Gleason's bulk, Wilt Chamberlain's height.

4. Draw the face, either on paper or mentally. You don't have to be an artist to use the outstanding feature to sketch a cartoon of the person you've just met. Actually, the cartoon is not really a picture. But because a cartoon can greatly exaggerate the special

features of the person, it is easy to recognize him. If you've put the cartoon down on paper, don't be embarrassed. You won't have to show it to the person you've just met.

5. Compare the mental or drawn cartoon with this person the next time you see him or her.

6. Redo the cartoon after you've compared it with its model. You will find that your ability to make a picture (mental or actual) will increase with practice.

Another good exercise along these lines is to stop for a few minutes and think about three or four good friends. What are their key features? Mentally cartoon them. Now practice with several fellow employees. If you want to see how good you can become, mentally cartoon such famous men as the President, the mayor of your town, or some such person, so that you can check your own cartoon with those of the professional newspaper cartoonists.

Recalling That Name

Most of us have more trouble with names than faces. This is because of the way we meet people. He is introduced to us, or else introduces himself. In either case, we hear the name and see the face. Usually, the name is given only once. However, we are able to continue to see and study the face. That's why the face is often all too familiar, but the name just evades us.

Memory experts offer a four-step program to help us recall names:

1. Get the name clearly and correctly. Forget about looking over the person you are meeting, or thinking about what you were going to say until you have the full correct name engraved solidly in your mind. If the name is unusual or you failed to catch it, don't worry about hurting the person's feelings by asking him to repeat his name. In most cases, he'll be pleased that you think enough of him to get his name correct. You can bolster your recall by asking how he pronounces or spells his name.

2. Use the name at once in your reply. "I'm very happy to meet you, Mr. Gordon." Your new acquaintance has the chance to correct you if you have mispronounced his name. In any event, you've had the opportunity to further impress his name and face in your memory—and you've pleased him.

3. Repeat the name as often as possible in your conversation. Each repetition fixes the name more firmly in your mind.

4. Write the name down as soon as you can. Spelling it out on paper also acts to fix the name more firmly in your mind. Reread the name and practice pronouncing it. You might carry a small notepad or a sheet of paper around for this purpose.

Association Is a Major Aid

You must make every effort to make certain you will not only remember your new acquaintance's face, but also his name.

The experts say that the four rules we've just covered will help fix the name in your mind. Try connecting the name to one or more distinguishing factors, such as his appearance, occupation, or something that will have a special meaning to you. This is what we call "association."

Very simply, association permits you to form a mental picture in your mind of a person and an object or idea in such a way that you will find it almost impossible to think of one without thinking of the other.

That is not as hard to do as it may sound. Many names have another real meaning in English. Many foreign names have meanings, too. It does take time and effort to form these associations. But practice will soon make the job easy.

In some cases making an association is quite simple. Mr. Silver may have a full head of white hair. Seeing him from a distance will telegraph his name to your brain.

There are many common words to which we can associate names. For example, there are the Blacks, Whites, Greys or Grays, Greens or Greenes who associate to colors. Baker, Smith, Carpenter, Taylor, Wheelwright, and Shoemaker relate to occupations. We have

Mr. Spring, Summers, March and May to go with the time of the year; or such adjectives as Strong, Strange, or Small.

There are many other names that have a definite meaning or are descriptive to us. Fox, Lyons, Rice, Rivers, Lake are examples. Some people have the same name as a famous person and you can associate them with this person. The person could be a movie star, a sports figure, or a politician.

Those Difficult Names

Now, you may ask, "What about the more difficult names? The name that is not descriptive of anything?" The experts tell us to try to find an odd picture word that will jog our memory when we meet a person whose name falls into this category. If the word picture begins with the same letter, so much the better.

Here are a few samples:

Altman—Alter

Berra—Beer

Chesnow—Chestnut

Diesman—Diamond

Serif—Syrup

Siegel—Seagull

Mr. Groshans might have big hands. Mr. Nickel has a pleasant, round, almost coinlike face. How about Mr. Smith, the giant purchasing agent for the firm you've been trying to crack? You'll probably think of him as the big blacksmith who labored under the spreading chestnut tree, shoeing horses.

All this might sound ridiculous, but it isn't. These simple associations are often imaginary, but they do work. In fact, the more absurd your association, the more apt it is to work.

There is a good way to practice association. Look through a telephone book and select those names that have no meaning to you. Try to think up substitute names for these people. At first you might need a dictionary. After a little practice, this should be an easy game for you. Children do it all the time; most of us adults are just too lazy to try. You might try this as a car game the next time you take the family for a ride. Ask your children for the names of their classmates and see who can think up the best memory joggers for each name.

Just to review:

1. Try to visualize something with a meaning the same as the name.
2. If the name is the same as a famous person's, try to mentally picture the two together.
3. If there is no way to identify a person with a known something or person, find a word you can visualize that will help you to recall the name.

Meeting the Group

Now let's make it a little more difficult. Say you are attending a meeting or a convention. You walk into the hotel lobby or a suite and a friend calls you over to a crowd and calls out the names of everybody in his circle in rapid-fire succession. Most people would give up any attempt to remember each name and just grunt, "Pleased to meet you" to everybody.

But wait—remembering people you meet in a group is not really as tough as it seems. It does call, however, for harder work. Here are some of the ways to remember the names of people you meet in "large-size quantities" at gatherings.

1. Arrive early. This is one way to get a running jump on the future mob scene. You'll be able to wander about and meet people while they are still by themselves or are in smaller groups.

2. Get off in a corner by yourself every so often for a few minutes and repeat those names you're already heard. Scan the group to see if you can identify each of those people you've met.

3. Slow down the introductions to make sure that you do get the name correctly.

4. Sit down as soon as you are home and go over the names of the people you have met and try to picture each one. This is a good time to put association to work for you.

5. Spend a few minutes during each of the next

few days deliberately recalling the names of the people you met at the meeting.

Strengthening your memory calls for lots of hard work. But it is work that will pay dividends for you. You can remember names if you make the effort. Invest the necessary time to build your memory bank of names. It is one bank that will really pay off in satisfied customers and coworkers.

9

How to Profit by Listening

Listening is one gift that pays tremendous dividends, which unfortunately few of us really collect. We just don't listen as efficiently as we should.

In what other phase of your daily activities would you accept a 25 per cent level of efficiency? Yet, that is the level of listening efficiency for most of us. You can really see the waste when you analyze your working day and find that you may spend ten times as much time in listening as you do writing, up to five times as much as you do in reading, and from two to three times as much as you do in talking.

What's Hard About Listening?

Why is it so much harder to really listen than it is to read or write? For one thing, concentration in listening fights for attention against a feature peculiar to aural communication. The average rate of speech for most people is around 125 words per minute. This is considerably slower than your brain operates. What happens is that your brain has a good deal of spare time to loaf along or to devote to other subjects. This factor reduces the listening process of many people to a level of effectiveness far below what it really could be.

Listening Is an Art

Listening is really an art which offers several real benefits to you. First, as long as you are listening, you will profit in some way. You will learn something new or increase your present knowledge, or be entertained. Then, too, you gain the good will of other people. Generally, people prefer talking to listening. Every time you allow another person the opportunity to talk, he or she will become indebted to you.

There is a real danger, however, of permitting yourself to become a sounding board. In other parts of this book we've discussed how time can be wasted by idle chatter or gossip. Be as careful of lending your ear as you are of lending money.

What Causes Poor Listening?

For most of us, poor listening is caused by one or more of the following:

1. We are so busy trying to put our own ideas over that we don't bother to listen to what the other person has to say.

2. We are too lazy to listen. It is too easy to relax and just let the speaker's words flow right around us.

3. We fail to realize that we must make an effort to learn how to listen. And once we have achieved a good level of listening efficiency, we don't realize that we can only maintain it by staying in practice.

How to Hear More

Here are some suggestions which will help you to improve your listening efficiency. We'll elaborate on these as this chapter continues.

1. Think ahead of the speaker. Try to guess what he is leading up to. What conclusions will be drawn by him. In other words, try to anticipate what he will say.

2. Weigh the verbal evidence the talker presents to support his points.

3. Keep reviewing what the speaker says as your conversation continues.

4. Listen "between the lines." Search for the meanings the talker may not necessarily put into words. When a person talks, his words are only one part of his attempts to communicate with you. He uses gestures and expressions which he hopes will be significant to you. Usually these nonverbal messages will strengthen what he has to say. Sometimes, however, they may contradict his words. It is wise to watch these nonverbal actions because they sometimes may be more important than the words.

5. If you find it difficult to maintain your concentration at a 100 per cent level while listening, stop the speaker and ask him a question or two. His explanations will give you the opportunity to bring you back to full understanding. It will also assure you that you are getting a complete rundown of what you will be involved in.

6. You should practice concentration. Here's how: The next time you attend a meeting or convention, listen carefully to the speakers, but don't take notes. When they have finished, see if you can write a summary of what they said. Do the same when you listen to a speaker on the radio or television.

You might have your wife or a friend read a speech or a newspaper editorial to you. When they finish, write a summary of what you've heard. This practice will help you step up your powers of concentration. And that calls for practice whenever you have the time.

Get the Point

When a person talks to you, even informally, he usually tries to make a point. Sometimes in the course of his talk he makes several points, all of which add up to support his major position or idea.

A good listener tries to stay ahead of the talker by guessing what these points are before they are made. Whether you guess right or wrong, thinking like this pays off because you have forced yourself to concentrate so that you can analyze just what the talker is trying to tell you.

And, as mentioned earlier, you should also weigh and review what you have already heard. Such a review prevents your concentration from wandering. It is also wise to look for hidden meanings in what the other person is saying.

If you work at these mental activities, your ability to concentrate will certainly improve. And if it sounds like a lot of work, be assured that your normal thinking processes operate rapidly enough to provide you with ample time to perform all these mental tasks. Your mind is a wonderful instrument that can very rarely be overloaded.

Hear the Speaker Out

Another major obstacle to good listening is one which we may make ourselves. It is a reluctance to accept ideas different from our own that sometimes causes us not to listen.

The solution is to hear the speaker out. Withhold evaluation, judgment, and decision until after the speaker has finished. Then, and not before, review and make your assessment of his ideas. You should also hunt for the negative evidence—that is, ideas which might prove you wrong as well as those which prove you right. If you find yourself self-centered and inclined to consider others always wrong, you should force yourself to hear the other man out.

How to Profit by Listening

So much for building our understanding of the science of listening. Let's take a look at how good listening can help you in two of the most common phases of everyday business life—buying and selling. I don't care if you are an engineer, a research chemist, a school teacher, or a houseife; in one way or another, you are involved in buying or selling.

As a customer or prospect, one of the most common problems is that of protecting yourself against the high-pressure "sales pitch." It may be a product, a service, or an idea that you are exposed to. In such situations, the advantage is generally the talker's since he has at least three points working in his favor:

1. Time. If you are reading, you can reread and take the time to reconsider. A sales talk usually requires a quick answer.
2. An oral "sales pitch" is easier to give than a written one. This is especially true because a person usually doesn't listen to everything, and if his mind wanders, he may unconsciously lower his sales resistance.
3. Writers take greater pains with their words because their words are down in black and and white and can be checked and double-checked for accuracy. In contrast, unless there is a tape recorder available, a talker can color his words in any way he wishes. Exaggeration is a key tool of a high-pressure salesman.

Two Types of Persuasion

You'll usually find that a person trying to sell you something will use one of the two types of persuasive talks. He may even make an attempt to combine them.

The first type is a low-pressure one, designed to allow you to think you will be able to make a choice after weighing the evidence. The speaker spreads out both the facts for and against his proposal. As he concludes, he sums up and appeals for your support of his position. If your listening is at peak efficiency, you can weigh the pros and cons of the proposal and make a decision.

Evaluation is much more difficult in the second type of persuasion. The speaker may not provide all the facts. He may use many emotion-arousing devices to place his story favorably before you. He may be unethical enough to leave out or misstate evidence. He may resort to name-calling, name-dropping, false testimonials, or a "band wagon" appeal.

To be fair, this second type could be for a worthy cause as well as bad. The decision is entirely up to you. You do have a defense against this type of proposal. You should refuse to jump to conclusions, and request time to test the evidence. If you must say something immediately, let it be "No."

Four Tests for Evidence

There are four tests which you can give to the evidence presented in a persuasive speech. Try these to help you make your decision:

1. The test of time. Take a close look at the evidence if it is old and possibly outdated. What was right yesterday may not really be valid today.
2. The test of competency of the source. Make certain the talker knows what he is speaking about.

3. The test of prejudice. Is the speaker really neutral? More than likely he is prejudiced.
4. The test of completeness. Has the speaker given you all the facts? If not, why not?

How Listening Helps Selling

So much for your role as a buyer. Now, how can listening improve your salesmanship? There are a number of ways in which listening plays a part in the art of sales persuasion. If you do a genuine job of listening, asking questions, and listening to others, you will actually be putting yourself in the other fellow's shoes. This is one of the key reasons for the success of most salesmen. If the customer feels that you know and understand his needs and problems, he will be definitely more friendly toward you.

On the simplest level, listening can serve as a means of learning the customers' needs and problems in relation to what they want to buy or are going to be asked to buy.

The "listen before you act" approach to selling is built around a central question: How can you sell yourself or your product if you don't know what the prospective buyer wants and needs? This is a very simple premise. Unfortunately, it still remains unrecognized by many who sell.

Don't Stop Listening

You should never cease your aural study of the people with whom you must deal. As they talk, you should note with care both what they say and what they don't say. The way they skirt an objection may reveal their true feelings. So keep looking beyond the mere content of what you hear.

Properly used, the skill that is listening will be a strong tool to help you achieve success.

10

Thinking Your Way to the Right Decision

You can think your way to greater success in your business and in your everyday life. The key is simply to train your mind to utilize the creative potential you possessed when you were born and to use a simple six-step formula you'll find later on in this chapter.

The ability to think straight is an important asset to any person who must make decisions. And decision making is not limited to businessmen and women. You make decisions every single day of your life—choosing a new suit, buying a home or car, joining a club, going to a show, choosing what to have for dinner.

There is a definite map to making decisions, but before we examine it, let's take a look at the thinking process. We can define "thinking," for our purposes, as the careful and diligent efforts to discover methods of resolving the difficulties that face us in the everyday course of our lives.

Making decisions would, of course, be much less

of a chore if you could be sure that your decisions would not kick back. It is fear of failure, the consequence of guessing wrong, that often makes the decision-making process such an ordeal. Yet, this emotional strain can be reduced if you have a better understanding of what a decision is and if you learn how to protect your decision against failure.

Two Kinds of Decisions

Most of us in our everyday work deal with two kinds of decisions. We could call them the routine and the major decisions. In the routine, the conditions of the situation and the requirements which the solution has to satisfy are known to us. Our job is simply to choose between a few obvious alternatives. The basis for our judgment is often economy; and the decision is one that will accomplish the goal with a minimum of effort and disturbance.

Major decisions are something very different. They involve us to the extent that we must either find out what the situation is or change it—either finding out what the resources are or what they should be. Among your major decisions are those affecting productivity of a business, revamping an organization, large capital expenditures, training of salesmen and others, realignment of routes or districts, plant layout, and the flow of paperwork through an office.

In major decisions the important job is not so much to find the right answer as to find the right question. There is nothing so useless as the right answer to the wrong question.

And it is not enough to find the right answer. The course of action decided on must be put into effect. Management of a business, a club, or a home is not concerned with knowledge, but with performance. Nothing is so wasted as the answer which goes nowhere or the solution that is sabotaged by the people who could make it effective.

Dealing with Unknowns

No system can ever lead you inevitably to a correct decision; you'll always face unknown or unanticipated elements. Suppose you are the sales manager of a company and you have to select from a group of job applicants a very promising candidate for training in a key position. Your choice proves to be enthusiastic and eager, and everything moves nicely for the next few months. Then his wife inherits a large sum from an unexpected source and wants him to go into business for himself. Your months of training go out the window.

Let's find another example at the housewives' level. Say you are P.T.A. president and assign responsibility for a special event to a woman who has always done hard work in her committees. Unbeknown to you her husband is expecting a transfer and a promotion. Since this woman expects to be gone by the time your event rolls around, she unconsciously slows down and does very little planning. Just before your event, she moves and you are left holding the bag.

There was nothing wrong with either of these appointments, even though later developments proved them to be "wrong." You can never anticipate all eventualities. But within the limits of chance, you can improve your decision-making score—and with it your willingness to make decisions and to be decisive in all matters.

Three Rules of Decisiveness

The most important rule in decision making is to act decisively. Decisiveness is a habit which may be acquired if you follow religiously these three rules:

1. Decide all the small matters promptly.
2. Select your decision and forget the alternatives.
3. Put your decision into action.

Very rarely will you be asked to make decisions impulsively. But don't be afraid to make a mistake. Right or wrong, make a decision as soon as you have pursued the process of reaching a decision. And whatever decision you make should be a valid one, not merely an escape from the responsibility of making a decision.

Many a decision made from sheer fright is just a wild grasp in any direction. A man who has held back from making a decision until conditions just won't let him procrastinate any longer may find that the best solutions are no longer open to him. He may also find that he must now act without being able to give proper consideration to his problem.

The Decision-Making Process

A formula for making decisions was mentioned earlier. Here are the six steps that make it up.

1. Properly identify the problem.
2. Gather all available data.
3. List all possible solutions.
4. Test all possible solutions.
5. Select the best solution.
6. Put your decision to work.

After you analyze these six simple steps you will see that most of your past attempts at decision making have included these six basic actions, whether you realized it or not. You probably just didn't give the right names to what you have been doing. These six steps are normally followed in the order given, though the sequence can vary. Often you are already gathering data while you are trying to isolate the big problem. At other times you will be working at more than one phase at a time.

Properly Identify the Problem

What appears at first glance to be the elements of the problem seldom are the really important or relevant things. They are at best symptoms, and often the most visible symptoms are the least revealing ones.

A clash of personalities may be the result of poor organizational structure. An apparent problem in manufacturing costs may really be an engineering mistake or one in sales planning.

The first chore, then, is to find the real problem and to define it. This is not a matter for haste, but for careful inspection and deliberation. Definition of the problem cannot be accomplished until the element or elements are found in the situation which must be changed or acted upon.

Actually, you are halfway to a solution when you can write out a clear statement of your problem. This is often a tough job in business because few problems appear in truly clean-cut form. For example, suppose you find production behind schedule in your plant. You also know that you have been plagued with many absences. What is your real problem? Is it cutting absenteeism, or are the absences a sign of low employee morale? When you've carefully analyzed your problem, you may find it is "how to raise employee morale," not "how to improve production."

Careful study is necessary if you are to define properly your real problem. Sometimes you'll discover that the major problem is really made up of several smaller ones. These should be isolated and treated individually.

When you have found your real problem, write it down in as simple a way as possible. This will now act as a guide to help you keep your mental processes on the right track. Once this is done, you are ready for the next step.

Gathering All Available Data

The next step requires you to collect all the information you can that pertains to your problem. Obtain every possible fact and figure that is available. You will rarely see a man who has all the facts make a mistake because he knows too much.

Suppose you decide you want to take up the game of golf. You'll want to know where you can play, where and how you can learn to play, what equipment and lessons will cost you, what other expenses you could have. With this information on hand, you will then go ahead and decide if you want to pursue the hobby.

You should organize your collection of facts into some form that will permit you to make sense of them. One of my business friends carefully lists each fact on a separate file card before starting the decision-making process. He then discards those cards he feels will not provide an answer. Another man rules a sheet of paper in half the long way and lists the facts on the left side. As he studies each, he notes its relative importance and meaning on the right side.

Both the cards and the list are simply ideas for small businessmen or for everyday family use. In the larger businesses or corporations, charts and graphs and reports are made up to help with the decision.

One of the best ways to gather reliable data is to get out in the field and see what is going on for yourself. An oil distributor was faced with the problem of low gallonage delivered per truck mile. It took him only one morning to find out the reason for his problem.

He learned that his drivers loaded their tank trucks in the morning, using the time the fuel oil was being pumped into the tanks to gossip. About an hour after they finally left the plant, they all met at a diner for coffee and a chance to kid a good-looking waitress.

The solution was the institution of a new rule that all tank trucks must be filled every night. A morning and an afternoon coffee break were allowed, but each driver was to call in on his two-way radio when he was taking the break and let the dispatcher know where he could be reached. The long hauls over to the favorite diner were ended with the rule that coffee breaks were to be taken at the eating place closest to the last delivery.

Knowledge of the facts permitted a simple and profitable solution to the problem.

List All Possible Solutions

We start getting creative when we develop possible solutions to the problem that faces us. Here is where you should let your imagination have free reign to seek and offer new ideas to you. It is wise to write down every solution you come up with before you start to analyze and discard. Even if an idea seems absurd, write it down.

It is amazing how many ideas you can develop to fit any one problem once you've set your mind to it. I attended a seminar on creative problem-solving at the University of Buffalo some years ago. Each of the group was asked to reveal a personal or business problem that was bothering him. The others would "brainstorm" and offer solutions.

One of the youngest in my group was the son of a wealthy dairy owner. After training summers in different departments at the dairy, he was to start working full time in an executive position when he finished college. He was concerned that there would be friction when he moved in and the old-timers suddenly faced a new "unbeatable" rival.

Our group "brainstormed" ninety-six different ideas to help that young man!

You won't have a group to help you, but this is an example of the many possible solutions that can exist for a particular problem.

How long should you gather and study data?

Only as long as you can get something new from the information you have.

An added tip: After you have carefully analyzed all facts and listed your possible solutions, sleep on it! You can do this by actually going home and shutting up shop for the day, or you can shift over to another project that is completely different for an hour or two. Come back in a few hours or the next morning to choose the solution or solutions to be tested.

Test All Possible Solutions

You must try to be as objective as possible when you are testing the solutions you've come up with. If you are not truly objective, you may put aside judgment and select a solution you particularly favor, even if it is the wrong one. One way to help yourself be objective is to measure each solution against a guidepost or yardstick.

Each of your solutions could be studied in the light of the following:

1. Will this solution solve our problem?
2. Will this be a permanent or a stopgap solution?
3. Will the solution work in actual practice?
4. How much will the solution cost?
5. Can I, or the company, afford the cost?
6. Will all affected people go along with the solution?

Select the Best Solution

The true job of an executive is to make the final decision. It is a decision you have to live with and sleep with. Occasionally, one solution will stand out head and shoulders above the rest. If this is the case, you are lucky.

Sometimes, however, you may find that no one solution has come through all of your tests with a passing grade. The best choice may actually be a marriage of two or more of your solutions. Here you must gather together the strongest points of each of the solutions that will be used. Use your imagination together with your innate management skills to make the final decision.

Another word of advice here. The greatest problem is the temptation to let thinking be guided by desires or emotions. The following seven rules will help you keep your thinking logical:

1. Avoid quick decisions. Refuse to accept any solution until you have arrived at it by a step-by-step process.

2. Eliminate as much as possible any emotional influences.

3. Relax your mind, because you come up with distorted views and tend to take short cuts when you work under heavy pressure.

4. Study again any one solution or decision that seems too much in line with your own wishes.

5. Give your first solution a double check to see if it really is the proper one.

6. Think and think some more about your problem and its ramifications so that you do not take impulsive action.

7. Understand that the facts must be followed, even if the decision will be one that is distasteful.

Put Your Decision to Work

"Scientific" decision making has one last stage—putting your decision to work. If it works perfectly, you know you've made the right decision.

If the problem doesn't disappear after you made all allowances for any unforeseen difficulties, you'll have to go back through the decision-making process again. Perhaps now that you have seen what difficulties arise, another of your solutions will stand out as a better one.

Be absolutely certain that you did not define the wrong problem. Earlier it was said that the important key was to pick the right problem. Your choice could have been unsuccessful only because it was developed for the wrong problem.

People Are Most Important

Remember, no decision can be any better than the people who have to carry it out. A course of action may require more competence and understanding than the people involved may have, and yet be the only possible solution. If this is the case, you must provide in your decision for the efforts needed to raise the ability and standards of the present staff, or else find the new people who do have what it takes.

A perfect home-front example can be found in my own religious congregation. The major problem had been to gain sufficient publicity for the group's events and programs. Finally, the secretary checked over the membership cards and found that several men including myself were in public relations work. We were invited to come to a special meeting and offer advice. We quickly entered into the overall planning and promotion of all activities. It was a release and hobby for us. If we hadn't been asked to help, we would probably have never considered offering our services.

As a decision maker you can define, classify, assemble, set objectives, and select the solution, but you cannot supply the one ingredient needed to convert a solution into a decision—*action*. You only can communicate to others what they should be doing and motivate them to do it. And only as they take the right action is the decision actually made.

The participation of others in preliminary phases

of decision making may not be necessary and in some cases is actually undesirable. In many other instances, the people charged with carrying out the decision should take part in the work of developing alternatives. This may help in the final decision, because they can spot hidden difficulties and uncover overlooked resources which they know about because of their closeness to the situation.

And as a final suggestion: Because the decision affects the work of others, it must help them achieve their objectives, assist them in their work, contribute to their performing more effectively and with a greater sense of achievement. Decisions cannot be merely for the maker's benefit and his own satisfaction.

Modern business makes it highly important that every manager understand the process of decision making. You should understand these tools and their limitations, and also when to call on outside assistance.

Once you understand the basic methods involved in decision making, you will find yourself less likely to resort to gimmicks. Straight thinking will help you chart the right course in the uncertain sea of business competition, which is getting rougher for the unskilled with every advance of technology.

11

How to Profit from Your Mistakes

Running a busines provides many opportunities for making mistakes. To be really successful, a businessman must be decisive rather than cautious. We discussed this in the last chapter.

In today's tightly competitive world, the man who delays or fears to act has made an even bigger error than the one whose decision went wrong. But the successful man or woman is the one who tries to do something about his mistake. He must admit to errors. More important, he must undo them whenever possible and profit from his errors.

First, recognize that a mistake does not mean the end of the world. Realize that failure comes because of:

1. Misjudgments
2. Imperfect planning
3. Inadequate implementation

How to Undo Mistakes

Second, act to undo the mistake and see that it does not happen again. In most cases this calls for a four-part program:

1. Analyze your mistake.
2. Consider the cause or causes.
3. Prepare new plans of action.
4. Seek to benefit in some way from your error.

Analyze Your Mistakes

Before you can do anything about your mistake, it must be analyzed from your first idea to your last action. This will help you find out just why you lost out. Here are some guideposts for error analysis.

1. Was the error really important?
2. How was the error made?
3. Can you be certain the error will not recur?
4. Had your plans been really suitable for the project?
5. Was the timing of your action suitable?
6. Had you anticipated all eventualities?
7. Did you make an effort to check progress?
8. Did you have the right personnel to do the job?

9. Did your people have the proper information?
10. Did your people have the proper tools?
11. Did you or another adequately supervise your plan?
12. Was communication between all parties satisfactory?
13. Was the project completely followed up so that all data available was obtained?
14. Was top management 100 per cent behind the plan of action?
15. Was the action one that was stopgap?
16. Was the action one that was overly favored by you over other courses of action?

Consider the Cause

There are many reasons for errors. These include the lack of information, carelessness, misunderstanding, poor communications, and acts of God. Three oil distributors I know are perfect examples of having met these causes. Heavy investments in bulk storage and new delivery equipment became a financial hardship to one because unseasonably warm weather wrecked a heating season.

Another distributor invested heavily in two new service stations, only to find that the highway commission decided to build an alternative route. This was simply an error of carelessness through his failure to seek information on new road construction plans.

A third jobber assigned a ne'er-do-well brother-in-law to manage one of his branches. He knew the man drank and was undependable, but agreed to the move to soothe his wife. Within six months many customers were alienated, employees' morale was nonexistent, and the till had been tapped to make up gambling losses.

Prevent Recurring Errors

Once you've made the analysis, make certain that you act to prevent your error from happening again at some future time. When you have satisfied yourself that you know all the reasons for failure, you are ready to take the next step. This is insurance that the error or similar ones will not recur. If possible, try to set up a procedure that guarantees permanent elimination of the trouble.

For example, the man who mislocated the service stations should make certain he has all sources of information about road-building plans for the future. The man who over-financed storage and delivery equipment could seek better credit terms or methods of financing in the future.

We all know that the distributor with in-law trouble should exercise closer control over his hiring, but just how do you placate the wife unless you really put your foot down? If he is forced to hire the wrong man (such as a brother-in-law again), he must put the man in a position that will not affect the people who are important to the business—both customers and employees. He should also plan to maintain a closer watch over the relative's actions.

In general, the reason for the mistake or error dictates the action. If an employee is involved, additional training could be an answer. Unanticipated developments can be kept to a minimum if safeguards are set up to provide warning signals. A system of rechecking can also be set up.

Action After the Error

Once you know all the facts, you are ready to admit your mistake and to make new plans to run your business or to do your job. At this time it might be well to digress a moment and look at the position of an employee who has made a mistake. This would be an employee at the management or supervisory level.

Once he clearly understands why and how the error happened, he should admit his error. The man who doesn't may soon find himself involved in a maze of lies from which he cannot extricate himself.

There is a definite factor in your favor. Admission of an error does not have to be done in a negative manner. The employee should take advantage of what he has learned from the error to transform his report into a constructive one.

He should think in terms of his boss's reaction. He should not waste the boss's time by long, involved reports about why an error happened. He shouldn't overplay his anguish about making a mistake.

Very simply, the man who works for another should realize that his boss wants to know that something has happened that has caused certain other actions, and that his employee has taken steps to solve the problem. The report should be brief and factual.

Re-evaluating Programs

When you are satisfied that you fully understand the reason for the failure, it's time to act. First decide if you want to repeat the action or program. Can you use the same approach or one only slightly revised? In any case, your analysis of failure will point out which weak spots must be strengthened if the program is to be reused or modified.

Secondly, the reasons for the error may show that substantial changes must be made in the plan. You may have to consider firing some people and hiring new personnel. It might be necessary to purchase new equipment. New methods of operation, new procedures, revised timing may also be dictated.

Salvaging Poor Actions

There is a third alternative to either repeating or revising your earlier programs: a salvaging operation to prevent your first program from becoming a complete loss. After all, any action you did take has paid off at least by what you have learned from it.

What you have learned from your error or mistake can be used to point up weaknesses in your operations. Eliminate these, and your experiences will pay off in knowledge invaluable in your future decision-making actions.

Taking New Action

Now you are ready to move your business or your career ahead to new profits and greater success. This calls for several policy-making actions.

1. Take a new look at your goals and purposes.
2. Search for new techniques.
3. Make your new plans.
4. Look for the bugs in your new plans.
5. Assign the proper people to the job.
6. Prepare a definite schedule.
7. Start your new plan rolling.
8. Follow up to see that the plan is working properly.
9. Revise or modify your plan as necessary.

Never Ignore Mistakes

The most important rule for errors is that they should never be ignored. Despite the irritations and frustrations of failure, mistakes, and errors, remember that the ability to benefit from these setbacks can lead to greater success. Careful analysis of the failure points out the areas of weaknesses and often reveals unknown strengths. You can profit from failure by asking such questions as:

1. Can the causes of failure be eliminated?
2. What ideas, experiences, or techniques can be salvaged from the mistake?
3. Does the failure provide evidence of other activities that should be re-examined?

Make certain that all facts affecting the failure and the causes are studied and measured. If the errors are just forgotten, they will grow larger. No matter what the mistake is or whatever the circumstances affecting it, the failure must be subjected to the same careful analysis that precedes any decision.

It is taken for granted that each of us will err at some time. Your success is really rated on what you do to undo your mistakes and to profit from them.

12

The Art of Trouble Shooting

Our historians have always managed to assign a name to a period of time. They have come up with such graphic ones as "Dark Ages," "Renaissance," and "Industrial Revolution." In the future they will probably label our own era "The Aspirin Age." We seem to be a race beset by problems in our business and everyday life. It has been said that we down more than 10,000,000 pounds of aspirin every year as a result of these problems.

In Chapter 10 we discussed decision making. There is no doubt that every problem requires that we make a decision as we attempt to ease our worries. But not all actions requiring decisions are problems, even though many decisions saddle us with problems. Our social and business environments continually breed problems that require fast action. These may be problems in dealing with people, with equipment, or with products or services. Our success in solving these problems can be helped by the simple problem-solving formula that follows in this chapter.

Caution: Separate Worry from Problems

Worry can be defined, for our purposes, as a combined physical and emotional tension that creeps over a person who is perplexed. To solve a problem quickly, you must first overcome worry. For too many of us, worry acts as a substitute for figuring things out. It is the deadly enemy preventing us from thinking straight.

You can overcome worry if you form strong mental patterns that will take over automatically and begin to solve each problem as it occurs. If you achieve this, your built-in problem-solving habit should take over one-two-three just as automatically as when you slide behind the wheel of your car and instinctively begin to drive.

Prevention Is the First Step

The easiest way to solve a problem is to try to prevent it from happening in the first place. If you want to prevent trouble with your house, your car, or your heating unit, you see that these items are checked and receive good service. In a business this is called preventive maintenance.

Problem-Solving Formula

The formula for decision making had six steps; there are four in the formula that will help you act fast as a trouble-shooter of your problems:

1. Get all the facts and define your problem.
2. Weigh the facts and decide what to do.
3. Act on your solution.
4. Measure your success.

Define Your Problem

The first step is to define and clarify your problem so you'll know exactly what you are trying to solve. Just suppose you are driving your wife to the store and your car stops dead. You look first at the gauges in your dashboard, and you discover that you are out of gasoline. All you have to do is to find a way to refuel your car. But suppose you have plenty of gas. Now you have to look further to find out why your car will not run.

The more facts you have, the easier your problem solving will be. You can handicap yourself if you try to solve your problem before you have a sufficient understanding of what is going on. So step number one, again, is to get the facts . . . *all* the facts.

Weigh the Facts

You must have the complete story so that you can review the problem and see what rules or policies apply, and talk it over with other people if necessary. With these facts well in hand, you are ready for step number two.

All the facts and information you have gathered must be made to fit together, or else be discarded. You now weigh each fact in your mind and come up with one or several possible courses of action.

Many times there will be more than one possible solution. Here your past experience comes in handy. Follow the action suggested by what has most often proved successful in the past.

If you can find no action that has been successfully used before, you must consider carefully the possible effect of every possible solution on all people involved.

What you have actually done is pieced all the facts together, considered their relationship with each other, checked to find precedents, decided what to do, and tried to estimate the effects of your actions on your business or environment, on other people involved, and on you yourself.

Act on Your Solution

With your groundwork completed and your decision made, you are ready to put your solution into action. The assembly and consideration of all the facts, the weighing of the facts, and the actual decision are merely motions that accomplish nothing until you actually put your solution to work.

The action may involve only you, or you may need the assistance and participation of others. If you were going to act to have a neighbor remove his fence from your property, for example, you would need the help of a lawyer.

Even when you decide to act and start the ball rolling yourself and then utilize the assistance of an expert, such as a lawyer, you have not completed the problem solving until you have decided who will do the necessary work, how much each will do, and when each will do what is expected of him.

Measure Your Success

Even now you are not finished. You still have to complete what is probably the most important step in our trouble-shooting operation. You must check the results of your action. If everything is moving along, fine! If the problem still exists to some degree, you must completely re-examine the whole solution and find out what went wrong, or just what you failed to do.

Your follow-up should begin almost immediately after you put a solution to work. This follow-up should be a continual process until you are firmly convinced that you have solved your problem. If you are dealing with people, you will have to watch their actions closely.

A man or woman who can trouble shoot will quickly gain the reputation of a person who can be counted on. If you are working for somebody else, your boss will realize your abilities and potentials and your advancement should be assured. If you have your own business, the men who supply you merchandise and products, the bankers who supply your money needs, and the friends and neighbors who need help and guidance in community activities will all come to respect you and look to your leadership.

Working with Others

13

How to Be a Good Communicator

From the president of a nation or a business on down, communication is the primary job of every man or woman who aspires to business or social success.

If you want to get things done, the key to your success is the ability to use that all-important tool—communication. As much as 80 to 90 per cent of an executive's time is spent giving or receiving ideas, instructions, decisions, or plans, and trying to obtain understanding.

Communication can be accomplished in two ways: through the spoken word and by writing. This chapter will cover the basic principles of communication as well as the art of speaking face-to-face. The following chapters will examine effective writing techniques and the preparation and delivery of speeches and talks.

Communication Skills Must Be Developed

Too many of us take communication for granted. We devote countless hours to developing our skills in accounting, or management, or science, or learning to play golf. But we do not take the time to develop our communication skills, even though our very success will depend upon how well we communicate.

There is no magic to learning how to be a good communicator. You know what ideas you want to communicate to others. Your problem is to find the proper words to say what you want to say so that others understand what you want them to do.

Organize Yourself

The first step to getting your ideas across is to know in advance what you want to say. You must organize your thoughts before you say anything. Then carry your instructions or descriptions logically from one point to the next. Carefully tie your different ideas together so that the people you are talking to are never confused.

If you think it easy to give an instruction to other people, try this simple test I saw conducted at a meeting of the Sales Executive Club of New York. Two men were invited up to the stage. One was stationed on one side of a curtain; the other stood on the other side and was supposed to tell his partner how to draw a not very complicated collection of straight lines. The audience was able to see the progress made by the "artist." It was amazing to see how difficult it was for the "instructor" to describe just what he wanted the "artist" to do. The finished drawing did not at all resemble the original.

To communicate, you must underline in your own mind the important thoughts that you wish to pass along in this meeting with other minds. Then you use every technique you can to achieve your objective.

One last suggestion here. Don't try to throw too many different ideas into one communication. It may confuse the other person, or give him the impression that you are quite confused.

Don't Preach When You Talk

Few people like to be talked at or talked down to. They want to be talked to as an equal. You can put your ideas across most forcefully and without arousing resentment if your tone is both courteous and considerate.

Use All Your Tools

When you are talking face-to-face, there are many little things you can use to put over what you want to say. These are simple techniques that you should put to work for you. They include your facial expressions, your eye movements, and the tone of your voice. Your choice of words and their "finer" meanings will also help you obtain the reactions you wish.

And speaking of tone, put pep into what you want to say. The flat lackluster tone of voice that moves stolidly along may very well put your listeners to sleep, because they give up trying to pick out the important points that you are trying to make. If you want to emphasize an important idea, raise your voice or lower it, whichever is necessary to underline vocally what you believe is important.

Try and Try Again

Suppose you can't seem to put your idea across. The answer is to try again another way. Adjust your methods to your listener. Your manner of speaking may even vary. You'll talk one way if you are trying to explain a problem, another if you are asking for information, and still a third way if you are giving a direct order.

You should try to pick the right words—those that will be understood by the person with whom you are speaking. If the other person fails to understand you, both of you are wasting time. Your objective is to use the words that mean the same things to both of you.

If you are not certain that you are getting across, repeat yourself. But try to say it another way. You might use an illustration or two to strengthen your original presentation.

Give as Well as Take

Don't do all the talking. Give the other person a chance to respond to you. Try to encourage the others who are listening to participate by slanting your conversation in such a way that they have to contribute. You can ask them questions. You can ask for suggestions. You can ask for their experience. When you express your interest in them, you can usually get them to take part wholeheartedly.

Try to give the other person some idea or benefit from your presentation. Look at everything from the other person's point of view and show him how he will benefit if he does what you advocate. And remember, it is just as vital to do this with people who work for you as it is with people at your level, or above.

Try Listening

Some of us have a bad fault. We forget that communication is a two-way street. It's more than just getting the other person to take part in the conversation. Some of us just stop listening when others open their mouths.

You must be attentive to your listener's every action. Watch faces, eyes, body movements. You can quickly discover if you have lost the listener's interest. And you must then listen to what he says in response and how he says it. When you discover how the other person is receiving your message, you'll be better able to put the emphasis on your words to put your message over.

When to Stop Talking

Once you finish, stop talking. Never underestimate the intelligence of the other fellow. If you continue to repeat yourself and your ideas, you take the chance of losing him and his interest in your proposal. The rule is to say it simply, say it fast, and shut up.

The Follow-Up Is Vital

The most expert communicator can fail if he does not follow up. Even under the most ideal circumstances, your thoughts may not be understood. Most people are just unable to absorb all of what they hear or read.

Your big problem is to find out just how much of what you said to another person is understood. The only way to be certain that your suggestions or orders are carried out is to ask the other person to repeat what you have told him. Ask him as many questions as necessary to let you know that he has understood what is expected of him. If he is doing a job for you, you can review his performance to see just how well he has really understood.

Psychologists tell us that the best way to make an impression on another person is to appeal to as many of his senses as you possibly can. One of the best ways to put your ideas over is to use visual aids to reach others through their eyes. You don't have to have expensive visual aids made up. A simple sketch or diagram, or even a photograph, will reinforce your oral instructions.

Your Voice Is Also a Tool

It may be possible that while your words are well chosen and your ideas easily understandable, you are not getting your story across for another reason. Your voice may be against you. It may be irritating or distracting to the people with whom you are communicating.

Stop for a second and analyze just what a voice means to you when you are listening to somebody else. Does a weak, hesitant voice indicate weakness or lack of confidence? Does a harsh voice give you the impression that the other person is arrogant and one you could dislike? Is the firm, cultured voice indicative of a confident, poised speaker?

Into which of these categories do you fall?

There is an easy way to find out, and you may be surprised at the results, because few of us actually would recognize our own voice if we heard it as others do. The best way to study your own voice is to obtain a tape recorder and to let it run while you are talking on the phone or to another person. Now play the recorder back. Do you note any of the following defects?

. . . a slurring or mumbling of words, or

. . . a lack of expression with a lapse into a monotone, or

. . . an unpleasant tone that may be too high, nasal, or breathless, or

. . . a lot of word pauses such as *oh* . . . *ah* . . . *mmm,* or other similar sounds.

Ask another person who is interested in you to sit down and listen to the tape. It may be your wife, an associate, or a good friend. Ask him to be frank and tell you what he really thinks, because you need his help.

You may find that you will need a speech teacher or expert to help improve your voice. Speech improvement assistance is available from many sources. Colleges, universities, and even high schools offering adult education courses offer speech classes. In many localities, organizations such as the Sales Executive Clubs run similar classes. There are also specialists who can be hired to help you. Many men have joined local chapters of the toastmaster organizations. Here they get the opportunity to practice their speech and to have other men with similar problems offer constructive criticism.

Speaking Rate Must Be Regulated

We can offer some tips to help you speak with greater clarity. Find the proper rate of speed that for you will ensure intelligible speech. If you speak too rapidly, you may slur your words. In contrast, a slow, steady rate of speed quickly becomes a monotone. Good speakers vary their speed as they talk. They often emphasize important points by pausing both before and after the major thought.

If you talk in a tone too low or too high, your listener may become annoyed. He'll definitely be distracted. When you talk to others, it's wise to pitch your voice at the same level they are using. Vary this pitch for emphasis so that you make it easier for them to listen to you and, therefore, to understand you.

The skills of oral communication can be improved through practice just as you can improve your golf game or your swimming. Once you have achieved the ability to communicate effectively, you have gone a long way toward assuring yourself both that you can get others to do what you want, and that you will be able to put your point of view over at all times.

14

Say It Simply When You Are Writing

Living and working in today's modern world, you receive and write more letters, memos, and reports than your counterpart did of twenty or more years ago. And all this writing can come back to haunt you at some future time. In speaking, your actual words virtually disappear into the air. In writing, however, anyone who wishes to can save what you have written for future reference. Writing, therefore, plays a big role in the continued growth of every one of us.

You don't have to be a professional writer to compose good letters, memos, and reports with a minimum of time and effort. But many executives seem to tense up when faced with the prospect of writing. They know what they want to say, but the process of putting their thoughts on paper seems to frighten them.

I hope that the simple rules I'll outline in this chapter will help make business writing easier for you.

Secure Favorable Response

First of all, remember that the basic purpose of any business message is to secure a favorable response from those to whom it is directed. If your message does not gain this goal, it is worthless, regardless of the time and effort you spent composing it.

A second fact to bear in mind is that your reader's time is very valuable to him, whether he is an associate, a superior, a supplier, a customer, or one of your subordinates.

Third, remember that you must write your message so that there is no possibility for you to be misunderstood. You can do this if you remember that any communication can be effective if it is accurate, is well planned and thought out in advance of writing, is clear and brief.

Here are four sound rules worth remembering:

1. Don't say anything unless you can back it up with facts. Inaccuracies will reflect upon your ability.

2. Plan your communication before you begin to write. Think out your idea. Assemble all needed data and arrange it in logical importance.

3. Write simply. Many people think that by using semilegal or impressive-sounding phrases they are giving the impression of education and importance. Nothing could be farther from the truth. These words tend to slow the reader down, and may often make it more difficult to understand what is wanted. Why say "here-

after and henceforth" when "in the future" is clearer? Why use "due to the fact that" when one word, "since," will suffice?

4. The importance of being brief is obvious. If you follow the three previous rules, there will be no need for repetition. Excessive wordage should be eliminated so that you save both your own and your reader's time.

The good writers are known for their brevity. For example, The Gettysburg Address contains only 266 words. The Ten Commandments comprise 297 words. The Declaration of Independence has only about 1,500 words.

There are two good rules to remember. First, before you take a pen in hand or begin to dictate to your secretary, ask yourself: "Is this message necessary? Do I have anything to say?"

If you must write, then, second: "Can I find a briefer, clearer way to say what I want to say?"

Writing the Business Letter

Successful executives budget their time and schedule certain of their activities for a definite time period of the day. Part of your daily schedule should include a time when you read your incoming mail, and a specific time for answering it.

Many men prefer to give their mail some thought before they answer it. This is advisable. They read their correspondence in the morning and dictate their replies in the afternoons.

As you read your mail, it may be advisable in some cases to jot down important points in the margin of the letter. This might include such matters as what information to have your secretary look up so that you can give an intelligent answer.

In planning your letter, you won't go wrong if you follow the excellent guide to good writing that has been established by our newspaper editors. They insist that their reporters tell them: Who, What, When, Where, Why, and How.

Another important point to remember is the tone of your communication. Too often, businessmen forget that their major stock in trade is their friendliness. You should try to make your friendly attitude readily apparent to your readers. You can do this as you write or dictate by thinking of the recipient as your friend. Not only will a friendly letter create a better impression with your reader, it will help place him in a receptive frame of mind.

The Mechanics of Writing

Too many executives are overly concerned with the mechanics of writing. Good English is important and you should strive for correct usage, else you show your ignorance or laziness. But there is no reason to become a slave of grammatical perfection. Some men and women become so involved that they pay more attention to periods, commas, and semicolons than they do to the message they are trying to communicate.

But it is nonetheless advisable to take a very brief look at the "signposts" that do direct our language.

To begin with, the semicolon's (;) main purpose is to signal a long pause or a change in thought, instead of a full stop that would be indicated by a period (.). It is often used instead of the word "and." For example: "You voted for him; I didn't; so what?" or, "I wrote last week; there has been no reply."

The colon (:) is a sort of signpost that points the way to the next thing you are going to say. For instance, "Here are three rules that you should follow: say it simply, say it fast, and shut up." Or, "There are three companies interested: Allied, General, and Imperial."

The comma (,) can easily be misused or overused. You can handle it without too much trouble if you bear one thing in mind. The comma denotes a short pause in a single train of thought. In action, a comma sets off items in a series: "We saw John, Joe, and Mary." A conditional sentence will also require a comma: "If I could, I would." Connective adverbs usually go between commas: "You, however, are mistaken." A comma will precede a person's identification: "John Rathbone, President of Allied Importers." A comma can lead into a quotation: She said, "Well, I think you could be right."

The question mark (?) hardly seems to need any explanation.

The exclamation point (!) I've heard very aptly called the astonisher. Example: "Wow! What an explosion!"

Parentheses ( ) and dashes (—) are all used pretty much for one purpose: to bring into a sentence additional or emphasizing material that is not *directly* connected with the sentence's topic. For example: "Sam Smith (our first president) started our company in that little one-room building." "That's the biggest—by far the biggest—generator available."

Quotation marks (" ") enclose what other people say. A single quotation mark (') encloses a quotation within a quotation. "She turned to me and said, 'I won't go.' "

The apostrophe (') has two main uses: (1) to make a noun possessive, for example, "The company's car," and (2) to indicate that you have omitted a letter or figure. Some examples are the contraction of cannot (can't) or "He is a member of the class of '68."

Punctuation marks are just little tools to help you clarify your sentences and make them easier to read.

Develop a Major Theme

The best business letter is one that is developed along one major theme. Once you have decided on your keynote idea, you must mentally visualize just how you will present it to the reader so that he will accept your proposal. The best way to do this is to place yourself in his shoes. Ask yourself such questions as, "What's in it for me?" "What has the greatest appeal to me?" "Why should I do what he asks?"

Once you have decided on your major theme and the tone you will follow, and analyzed just what is necessary to sell the other person on your point of view, you must gather all data that will supplement your proposal. This information should prove your case, and it should be pertinent and not distracting. A person has only a limited amount of mental power available at any given moment, and his brain can only deal with one matter at a time.

There are other factors which also tend to confuse the reader. Try to avoid the use of complex or strange words, long paragraphs, and long, involved sentences.

The All-Important First Paragraph

You are now prepared to dictate or write your letter and your next step is to decide what you will say in that all-important first paragraph. Many executives claim that preparing a first paragraph that will attract attention is their most difficult and time-consuming job. Actually, the problem is minor if you have thought about what you want to say and have all the necessary data available.

In a good business letter, your first paragraph should accomplish the following two purposes:

1. Inform the reader of what the letter is about.
2. Make a favorable impression on the reader.

There is no reason why the recipient of your letter

must scan through two or three paragraphs before he finds out what your letter is about. It is also extremely important that he form a favorable impression immediately. His attitude, as he reads the first few sentences, will more than likely affect his reception of the rest of your letter.

You utilize the body of the letter to expand your main theme and also include all necessary data to help prove your points. The final paragraphs are important because here is where you tell your reader what you want him to do and urge him to act. You have already outlined your case and supported it with facts. In the last paragraphs, you must clearly state what these facts prove and what you expect your reader to do.

As with every human endeavor, "Practice makes perfect." This is also true of letter writing. If you follow the ideas and basic letter outline suggested, you will find that before too many weeks have passed, you will be producing polished letters. Of course, the final judgment of any letter will always be: Did it satisfactorily accomplish the purpose for which it was written?

Some busy executives I've met have developed form letters that are supposed to handle certain types of inquiries or complaints. This practice is acceptable to a limited degree. However, the form letter should always be carefully studied before being sent out. You can never tell when a few minutes spent writing a personal letter will pay off for you.

Writing the Right Memo

Just as letters serve as a communication link with the general public and business acquaintances, another form of communication transmits information within a company. This form is the memo, a short word for memorandum.

The use of the memo has skyrocketed in recent years. This rise can be attributed to the fact that in today's complex business world, oral communication is no longer capable of doing an efficient job. Executives and their subordinates today must assimilate and retain a multitude of facts. Because of the pressures of time and competition, it is easy to forget details. A written memo serves as both a reminder and a semipermanent record that certain directives were issued.

Properly used, memos act as important links between management and other personnel, and materially assist in the orderly guidance and control of a business organization.

Informational memos have gained wide acceptance in business today as morale builders. Management has realized that a lack of information about company actions or events can lower the efficiency and morale of the workers. Good workers have an interest in their company and like to know how events and happenings will affect them. Informational memos can be used to keep employees fully informed on all policy changes and other company news.

Basically the rules of memo writing are the same as for letter writing. You should state the purpose of your memo in your first paragraph. This is followed in the body of the memo by a detailed discussion supplemented by the necessary data. Your final paragraph will contain the recommendations and should point out how the reader and his company will benefit if the recommendations are carried out.

Preparing Reports

Reports are used today in a wide variety of ways. They can cover the activities of one person; analyze the operations of a department or a company for a definite period; disclose the financial condition of a firm; investigate a new product or market; report on an operational problem; or suggest a change.

Most reports can be classified into two main categories:

1. Reports that relate to specific phases of operations and contain only facts.
2. Reports that analyze and present conclusions and recommendations.

The first category consists of mostly routine reports and describes the gathering of facts and presents specific details without comment.

The more complex analytical report not only reports the facts but also contains conclusions and recommendations. This report usually contains a study of both past and present activities and may forecast future happenings.

I've found that most bad reports are bad because the writer did not have a clear idea of what was expected of him. Here, the fault lies with him for not seeking clarification of his assignment, and also with the individual who assigned the project.

Accepting the Assignment

What should you do if you receive the job of writing a report? The following checklist will help you get properly started. Incidentally, if you have the responsibility of assigning a report-writing project to another, just follow the same list when you pass out the assignment.

1. Make certain the project and content have been clearly defined for you.

2. Find out if the project can be limited to certain specific areas.

3. Find out if you are expected to make recommendations.

4. Get a completion date for the report.

5. Find out why the report is wanted and what its value will be when it is completed.

6. Be certain that you know exactly what is expected of you before you begin the project.

You should take copious notes and ask questions when the project is being explained to you. Only by doing this can you be assured of doing the job expected.

Requirements for Report Writers

Let's take a look at some of the requirements of a good report writer. He should be accurate, since important decisions may be made on the facts contained in his report.

Resourcefulness should certainly be one of his strong points. There is usually a hard core of information readily available to us on most topics. The man or woman who is resourceful makes use of this information, and then goes a step or two further to seek all new data and new sources to complete his report.

The last requirement is plenty of patience. The process of gathering and examining large amounts of data, as well as developing new sources of information, can be tedious. But if you are diligent and use your intelligence, your efforts will be rewarded with a good, solid presentation.

Language and Form

The final decision on how a report is to be written will depend on both the topic and the audience. If your report is being written for one man, it can be prepared in letter form. If the report is to be published or circulated to a number of people, it should be prepared in a more formal form.

The language you use will depend on the type of document. If an accountant, lawyer, engineer, or other specialist writes a report, it is permissible for him to use technical language only if the report is being read by other men of the same background. If the report is directed at men without this background or to a wide audience, every effort should be made to cut the amount of professional terminology to a minimum.

Preparing the Outline

Assuming that you clearly understand your goal and that you have carefully assembled all the necessary data, your next step is to evaluate the material at hand. Examine all material for discrepancies and contradictions. Try to eliminate all data not directly relating to the problem at hand and summarize what remains.

Now, you should mentally review your material and visualize how it fits together. After you have done this, get your facts down on paper in the form of a written outline. This outline should contain an introduction, a main body, and a conclusion. This working outline should not be overloaded with details.

Writing the Report

Now you are ready to begin your writing assignment. Your introduction should state your purpose and the area covered by your report, as well as your sources of information. If your report is a lengthy one, it should include a summary of your findings and recommendations.

You should develop all the essential data for your report in a logical sequence. Long reports should have the subjects divided by certain topic areas. These can be subdivided if necessary. I strongly recommend that you use descriptive captions and subheads as reference points wherever possible.

After you have reported the results of your investigation and presented your supporting evidence, your final step is to present your conclusions. If you have been asked to make recommendations, do so, at this point. These recommendations should be formally supported by the facts contained in the body of your report.

You should use exhibits whenever they will improve your presentation. Exhibits can include photographs, tables, graphs, and maps. They should only be used if they will clarify the facts that you present. Nonessential exhibits should be avoided if their only use is to beef up the report. These will only tend to confuse the reader and detract from the text.

As we mentioned before, short reports can be

handled in letter form. Comprehensive reports should be arranged along the following basic lines:

Title page
Introduction
Table of contents
Body of report
Conclusion and recommendations
Exhibits
Bibliography

There is no easy way to write a business letter, memo, or report. However, you will find that writing is simpler if you follow the suggestions outlined and heed the rule that effective communications are *accurate* . . . are *planned in advance* . . . are *clear* . . . and *brief.*

15

How to Prepare and Give Better Speeches

Men and women who normally make decisions that affect their very future without a second thought are often turned into quivering wrecks when asked to say a few words.

Whether it's a keynote speech at a convention, a few words at a club meeting, or a report to company officials, the idea of standing on their two feet and stating their ideas throws them completely. Such fear is brought about only by lack of proper training.

The fear of talking on your feet must be overcome because talking in public is not the out-of-the-way event it used to be for the average man. It is a sign of a person's growing stature when the number of his invitations to speak in public increases.

Perserverance, Preparation, Practice

Three key words in becoming a good public speaker are perserverance, preparation, and practice. Public speaking requires that you be willing to work hard and devote time to learning how to do it. There are no simple short cuts for becoming a good speaker. Some people are born with the presence and the voice. If you were not one of the lucky ones, you can still acquire the skills.

You must be willing to spend time building your vocabulary. You must practice to develop a good speaking voice, and you must also try for orderly thinking. Whatever forcefulness or persuasiveness you are able to put into your speech will require careful preparation. And once your speech is written, you must work hard to perfect your presentation.

Your Obligation to the Audience

Any audience is important and you should remember that you have a definite obligation toward any group that has taken the time to come to hear you. Your speech must be both fitting and pertinent to the occasion. It should establish the fact that you feel your subject is important both to you and the audience. Never let your presentation drop below this level of interest. If you have thirty minutes allotted to you, give them thirty minutes of good, solid talk. Work hard to keep your pace high. You should think, speak, and act in terms of your audience's interests.

The first requirement of a speaker is that he have something to say. By this I do not mean that you can get up and say just anything. What you have to say must need saying.

Any speaker must know the task that has been set for him by those who invited him, and just how far it is his duty to carry his audience. The question facing you is not primarily "*What* am I to say?" but rather, "Why am I to say *this?* What special knowledge or experience have I to pass along to those who are here to hear me?"

You may not want to sell a product or an idea, win a vote, or organize a committee; but unless you set a target for yourself, a desired reaction from your audience, your speech will lack vitality. And your audience will quickly know this.

Building the Speech

Like a house, every speech has to be built. First, you need a foundation, and then a framework to support the body of your presentation. If what you have to say tells the facts relating to a problem or a situation in such a way that your audience can easily follow your careful "construction," and if they feel at the end of your talk the way you want them to feel, then you have done a good job.

Preparation of a talk requires that you obtain current, up-to-date, and interesting information on your subject. You develop this information into a logical order as you build your talk to gain the purpose you had in mind. First you develop an outline. Your next step is to fill in the outline with the facts and illustrations you have found through research, and with your own documentation and proposals.

Every speech has three parts: the beginning, the middle, and the end. In having this characteristic, the preparation of a speech is not unlike the writing of reports or letters we covered in the last chapter.

You should plan to use your introduction to warm up your audience to the purpose of your address. The body of the talk will then be used to develop the facts upon which your thesis rests. The conclusion is the place to bring your audience around to accepting your point of view, and to acting as you want them to act.

Your first three minutes are vitally important. Unless you capture the attention of your audience during this time, you may not gain their complete interest at any time. Your opening sentences should be written to attract a favorable response, gain attention, and to lead into the rest of your talk.

Make your enthusiasm at being invited to talk to this audience very evident. Smile at them. If you have a good anecdote, use it. Try to show them you are "one of the boys." Get the audience on your side.

And one big warning: Don't ever apologize for being there. If you had nothing to offer, you would not have been invited. It is fine to appear modest, but don't beg off giving them a good talk. Remember—*you* are the expert.

The Body of the Speech

Once you've caught the attention of your audience, you must hold this precious thing. You must impress them, convince them, and motivate them to act. If you are making a report to stockholders, a safety talk to the scouts, a presentation to a service club or any other audience, take one hint. Don't try to turn them into a rampaging mob through the power of your rhetoric. *Do* attempt to increase their understanding and comprehension so that they will act in the way you wish them to act.

Your speech should continually move forward, carrying the audience toward the conclusion you want to make. You can do this only by carefully planning your talk before you give it. Point out your intense interest in your subject.

Vary your pace. If you normally speak at a slow rate, prepare occasional paragraphs made up of both short sentences and staccato words. If you are a fast talker, inject longer sentences to slow you down. If you fail to do this, you may lose your audience.

When you make a point, build it up and stick to it. Every time you digress, you weaken your story, and may even end up losing your audience.

The Conclusion

Just as your first few words are vitally important, so is your conclusion. Don't leave your audience up in the air. Make your ending an effective stop. Too many times a fine talk is followed by an inane, "I'm sorry for taking so much of your time." It is better to say just "Thank you" and sit down. Of course, the best conclusion is one which leaves the audience on the edge of their seats, just ready to act.

Writing a good conclusion takes practice. But you will find it gets easier as time goes on.

Writing the Speech

Now that we've discussed the parts of the speech, let's delve into the actual writing. When you write a speech you should try to adhere to the following qualities: simplicity, good language, accuracy, and, of course, honesty.

Here are a few suggestions about what not to do. Don't write to display your vocabulary. If your audience doesn't know what you mean, you are certainly wasting their time as well as your own. As you write, keep asking yourself, "What does this mean?"

Your talk should contain simple, clear-cut ideas that will make your audience react to your proposals.

Try to have one solid fact and an illustration to back up each main element in your talk. The facts may be from your own experience or from other sources. An important thing is to have your illustration appropriate.

How to Be Persuasive

Every speech should be persuasive. You should do more than merely describe the action you advocate. You should arouse the audience's desire to follow your suggestions. You can do this by expressing the proposed action with enthusiasm, and well documented evidence.

The following outline will help you develop your presentation:

1. Show that a problem does exist.
2. Explain the essential elements of the problem.
3. Tell about any previous failures to solve the problem.
4. Describe your solution and the benefits it offers.
5. Show why your solution is the one best one.
6. Explain what you want the audience to do.

Sitting Down to Your Typewriter

I know people who can dictate or write a speech without any real effort. Few of us are that lucky. I know I have to work hard at it. The best way to start is to make notes as your thoughts on the subject come to you. Put these ideas down on paper at once so you won't forget them. I've found making an outline a real aid for the novice.

At this point you will find the following suggestions useful.

1. Think out your subject. Consider your audience and its previous knowledge and the best ways to reach them. How will your facts react on the audience?

2. Consider your opening in which you pinpoint your purpose . . . your main body, in which you make your points in an orderly and progressive way . . . and your conclusion, in which you re-emphasize your important points and appeal for the desired action.

3. Consider all sides of the question so that you can answer any questions the audience may raise.

4. Write your speech. Write as you normally talk, about 100 to 150 words per minute, and in the language you would ordinarily use in everyday conversation. See that your speech covers the time allotted for it, certainly no more.

Here are a lot of "do's" that will help give the "spit and polish" that a good speech needs.

Do use strong verbs.

Do repeat, but only for emphasis.

Do keep your sentences short.

Do use specific words.

Do write tight sentences when you need emphasis.

Do use the active voice whenever possible.

And some "don't's" to be considered:

Don't use incongruous figures of speech.

Don't split infinitives.

Don't use highflown, poetic-type words.

5. Edit your speech.

6. Practice your speech against the clock. Trim it or expand it to meet your needs.

Before You Give Your Speech

Before you stand up, you should be fully prepared for the job ahead. Whether you are speaking from memory, from notes, or from a fully prepared manuscript—practice ahead of time. There is nothing worse than an unprepared speaker. The audience can spot it in seconds. Rehearse, rehearse some more, and then rehearse again.

Dress is also important. Don't let your clothes distract your audience. The loud Christmas tie from your mother-in-law belongs in a closet, not on display on your chest before an audience. Extremes in suits or shirts should also be avoided. A simply patterned tie and a dark suit is best, although one well-known speaker on sales subjects uses a light grey suit and a bright red tie as his trademark. Your clothes should be designed to make you appear impressive. A white pocket handkerchief completes the picture.

If you are planning to speak from notes or a manuscript, make certain beforehand that the meeting committee provides a lectern. There is nothing worse than reading a speech with your head bowed to read the sheets lying on the table or held in your hands.

If you have visual aids, be certain the easel, camera, screen, or whatever is necessary is available before you are introduced. No interruptions, such as would occur if a chart fell down or if your slides didn't fit the projector, must be permitted to distract the audience from your presentation.

Your Introduction

While some masters of ceremonies like to prepare their own speeches of introduction, most are pleased to have the speaker give them a prepared one in advance. In this way you, the speaker, are assured of getting the type of introduction you want. Prepare a simple introduction and have copies mimeographed. Be safe: Even though you send an introduction ahead, carry an extra copy along in case the first one is lost.

On Using Notes

If you are planning to use notes or a manuscript, place it on the lectern before you are introduced to the audience. If you have a title page, turn this over and have page one ready. The simple act of unfolding a manuscript or digging notes out of your pocket is distracting and may get your speech off to a bad start.

A word of caution: Make certain the people who speak before you or introduce you do not walk off with your manuscript. This is one very embarrassing way to lose your brains.

Now you are ready to begin. Thank the man who introduced you and make certain that you get his name correct. Thank the audience for having you and compliment them in some way.

Physically, you should appear natural and relaxed, but don't drape yourself over the lectern. You can rest your hands on the lectern, but only rest them there. I've known top executives who become so tensed up that their knuckles become white with the strain of holding on to the lectern and they look ready to tear the furniture apart. And stand steady on your own two feet; don't keep shifting around.

Smile and Start Talking

When the introduction is over, smile and start talking. It is wise to talk a bit louder than the man who introduced you and certainly louder than your normal speaking voice. They came to hear you, didn't they? Keep your voice natural and don't go in for old-fashioned flowery oratory.

A word to the wise: Watch good speakers perform. But don't try to imitate well-known TV or radio commentators. An amateur immitation very rarely comes off. The speakers you should watch and try to imitate are those who specialize in talking before such business groups as the Sales Executive Clubs. You might see if there is a local toastmasters group and join for the experience and self-confidence you will gain.

Don't talk too fast. About 100 to 150 words per minute is the figure we gave earlier as just right. You can pace yourself by putting appropriate notes in your manuscript or by underlinings and markings in the margin.

Audience Contact

Don't make a clock or other inanimate item in the room, or even a single person, the object of your attention. Look the audience directly in its "face." Talk to one person and then to his neighbor. Swing your eyes across the entire group, stopping to talk to individuals in all sections of the audience. Appear to hold a conversation rather than give a lecture. Never turn your back to the audience. Communication on this personal level can put your audience in the palm of your hand.

While you are talking to your audience, watch for signs of restlessness. A yawn may call for more emphasis on your next point. Or it may be time for you to tell an anecdote. One of my friends frequently gives a lengthy technical film slide talk to male audiences. Every few minutes he flashes pictures of buxom nudes on the screen. His audience is wide awake and waiting after he's shown them that first attention-getting slide!

Radiate energy, but don't pace back or forth—that will distract the group. There are also other things that will distract your audience, too: Don't pull at your glasses or your clothes. Don't scratch your head or body or smooth your hair. These are nervous habits that should be done away with.

Using Your Hands

Your hands are very important speaking tools. Don't anchor them to the lectern. Don't clasp them behind you or shove them into your pockets. Let them hang freely. Use them to make points, but don't flail them about. Use only gestures that come naturally. Don't light up a cigarette and begin to smoke.

Don't repeat one motion or gesture over and over. Watch the gestures used by trained speakers. Practice them in front of your mirror. You'll find that these motions will become very natural to you after some practice.

Grammar and Enunciation

Good grammar is important. But let me repeat what I said earlier, about the actual writing of the speech. Be sure you do not talk above your audience's head. There is no faster way to lose their interest. Speak in everyday terms and you'll be understood. It is also important that you do not appear to be talking down to them. Show that you respect their intelligence.

Good enunciation is very important and slowing down your rate of delivery will help you pronounce your words properly. If you make a mistake, don't go back and repeat the sentence. Chances are your audience forgot it as soon as you began your next chain of thought, if they even noticed it in the first place.

Watch the competition. Stop if a waiter comes in. He'll get out much faster if he feels he has become the center of attraction. Don't pass out literature that goes with your talk as part of your presentation. You can have the materials already on the seats when the audience comes in, or get it to them after the speech is over. Actually, it is better to give the literature to them afterwards, because they are apt to start looking at the material in their hands as you start talking.

Using the Microphone

If a microphone is available, use it. Talk at your normal speaking level or a slight bit higher. Don't whisper into the mike. When the time comes to shout, step back a pace before you let loose. Don't hang onto the microphone and use it for support. If it is too high or too low, adjust it before you begin talking. Urge those in charge of the meeting to make certain that the microphone is working before the program actually begins.

Using a Manuscript

If you plan to talk directly from a manuscript, don't be ashamed and apologize for doing so. Remember all those famous politicians you've seen on television. They speak from prepared manuscripts, often flashed on a prompter the audience can't see. They do so because it helps keep them on the proper track.

Here are some suggestions that should help you to use a prepared manuscript. First of all, don't apologize to them for reading your speech. This is important. If you rehearse well before your appearance, chances are your audience never will realize that you are reading your talk. Rehearsal will help you deliver your prepared presentation at a normal speaking pace. It will also prevent you from lapsing into a dull monotone.

Practice tonal variations. Read as you would talk to another person. Dots, dashes, underlining, and capitalization will help guide your tone through the manuscript.

Your eyes should not remain glued to your manuscript. With sufficient practice, all you will need to do is glance at the first words of each sentence or the first sentence of each paragraph. Your eyes should bounce right back off the page and out to your audience. Maintain the personal eye contact mentioned earlier. Use gestures and take deliberate pauses.

A last word about working with a manuscript. Use

a clean copy and make certain that the pages are in the proper order before you start.

The Anecdote

Many people find it difficult to tell an anecdote or a joke as part of their speech. They fear the audience will not find the story amusing and that the silence will be embarrassing. It takes practice to tell jokes. As a tip, tell only short stories. Very few people can tell a long humorous story to an audience. The funny stories or examples you use should fit right into your talk. They should not be told just because you feel it is necessary to tell one. They should be used only to illustrate points in your speech. And when you do tell a funny story, pause and let the audience enjoy it. Otherwise, the next portion of your talk will be lost in the laughter.

The more speeches you make, the better you will become. This is true if you practice and seek to improve. Go to hear well-known speakers. Watch their gestures, how they emphasize points, where they pause.

Your job is to arouse an emotional response in your audience. The combination of careful preparation and practiced presentation pays off. When properly used, the applause is more than politeness. It spells thanks.

16

How to Get People to Do What You Want

Several years ago I spent a day with two men, one of whom was considering the purchase of a franchised food shop, the other a friend of his who already had one. The first man was trying to decide if he should invest his life savings in the business.

"Tell me," the would-be purchaser asked his friend, "is there one major point that is the secret of success in this business? Your place seems to run so smoothly."

His friend replied: "There is no secret. The answer is really very simple. It is just not easy to carry out."

"What is it?"

"Very simply, it's the ability to deal successfully with people. To practice what you could call good human relations."

Success is very often just that simple, whether you are your own boss or working for others. Whatever your job is or will be, there will always be people with whom you must work. Some people will have to be led. You'll have to work with others at the associate level. You'll also have to follow and work with any bosses who are over you.

This brings us to a very simple description of human relations. In plain language, it is the ability to get along with other people. It is also very much a part of this business of management we have been talking about. According to the American Management Association, "Management is the act of getting things done through people."

The Right Climate

Just how do we go about building good human relations? The best way is to build a climate or environment in which our associates will work with us, not against us.

There are two major keys to success in human relations. The first is to act and feel toward others as you want them to act and feel toward you. It is the Golden Rule. You may not think so, but your attitude toward others can be spotted by those who come to know you through working with you.

The second important key is your actual method of dealing with other people. When you know *how*, you can get others to do what you want.

Understanding Others

To be successful in human relationships, you must understand those with whom you are working. This is a very difficult task, because no two people are exactly alike. However, people do have certain needs, desires, and traits in common with other people. One fundamental requirement for effective leadership is a reasonable working understanding of what makes people respond. Once you have this knowledge, you will know what motivations can cause others to respond the way you want them to.

It's been said that all people have one or more of these four basic common denominators:

1. They want to be with other people and to be accepted by the group.

2. They tend to resist change. Habits form easily and most of us quickly become used to doing certain things in a certain way. If you want to change people's habits, you must do it in a gradual manner. This calls for patience.

3. Every man (and woman, too) wants to be important. It has been said that this is the strongest human urge. The key here is to try to see everything from the other person's point of view, as well as from your own.

4. Every person wants security and peace of mind. You can give this to him by making him confident,

by letting him know that you feel he is doing a good job.

But People Are Different, Too

There is probably very little difference between two people. But even the slightest difference is the biggest thing in the world. People differ in one or more of these three things: the way they think, the way they feel, and in their actions. Let's spend a moment seeing why these differences do occur so that we can better understand others.

The way a person thinks depends upon his intelligence, his education, and his ability to think logically. His feelings are regulated to a good degree by such things as his aggressiveness, his reactions to praise and criticism, and his so-called boiling point. His actions depend on his thinking as well as his physical strength and endurance, and his coordination.

It takes practice in observation and understanding on your part to be able to determine the differences in people. This ability to analyze others will be a prize asset in helping you work with and handle other people.

How to Motivate Others

Now that we know the so-called common denominators in people, there are still other elements to be understood so that we can motivate others. Some of those with whom we work will be affected by only one or two of these elements; others can be moved through the use and understanding of many.

Here are the things we should do to get things done by others:

1. *A person wants fair play for his efforts.* See that he receives it. This must be considered a primary consideration. Compensation ranks high on the list of things a person wants from his job.

2. *Every man wants to feel important in the eyes of his family, his fellow workers, and the general community.* You can give people recognition by praising them, by asking their advice, and by showing an interest in their working and, in some cases, personal lives.

3. *Give each person a clear definition of what you expect of him.* It is surprising how few men really understand just what is expected of them. One of the best first steps is to write out a job description for anybody working for you. In some cases, you should sit down with the man or woman in question and go over the job step by step.

4. *Give each person an opportunity to advance and to grow within the organization.* No one will work at top efficiency and give full loyalty if he feels that he has been cut off from advancement.

5. *Let each person know just how well or poorly he is doing.* You can best do this by setting standards of performance, by letting the man know just how he is doing, and by giving help when it is needed. Every person has to know that he is an appreciated, participating member of the team.

6. *Job satisfaction becomes a good deal stronger if a person knows just how his superior or boss will react in different conditions.* If a leader is flighty and emotional and frequently shifts his plans and policies, his men usually will be off balance and confused.

7. *Communication is important, and those working for a company will usually perform better if they know what is going on.* Several of our recent chapters were devoted to the importance and the techniques of communication. Certainly, one of the best ways to gain cooperation is to keep people informed so that they will know not only what is going on, but why it is happening.

Remember, also, that communication is a two-way proposition. It is also a flowback or feedback of ideas, suggestions, and opinions from those who work for and with you. Learn to be a good listener and try to evaluate what you are hearing from your people.

One of the best ways to keep the two-way street called communication open is to establish and maintain friendly relationships with others. Take advantage of every opportunity to talk to them. Such events as vacation selections, pay raises, and job instruction are good ways to start. You can create other opportunities by making it a habit to say hello when the employee returns from vacation or sickness, by meetings in the lunchrooms, calls when an employee is in the hospital or sick at home, and by showing a sympathetic interest in the other person's personal problems.

8. *Delegate responsibility and authority to others, thus leaving you time to plan.* Try to have all decisions in your business made at the lowest possible level at

which information is available. In this way you have freed your time for more important activities.

In delegating, it is wise to let your subordinates know that their whole future does not depend upon how well they handle this one job. Also assure them that you will keep in touch, giving them the opportunity to report both progress and problems.

9. *When you must criticize, do it constructively and in private.* Get all the facts and review them with the man involved. Offer suggestions that will help him avoid making similar errors in the future. A tip here: Before you criticize, see if you can give the man a bit of praise. Another suggestion, and a very important one: Give your reprimands in private.

One of my earliest bosses had a habit of publicly criticizing and crucifying his subordinates. I was just out of college, but I can still vividly remember top executives making five to ten times my salary mercilously berated with the whole staff gathered around and the typing pool only a few feet away. It was of no wonder that his people were afraid to come up with ideas and that the rate of turnover was always high.

10. *Praise and give credit where it is due.* You can raise the morale and build the self-confidence of your men by giving them praise and recognition for a job well done. Another tip here: While you criticize in private, give your praise in public.

Remember, too, that giving a subordinate credit pays off twice. Not only does he receive recognition, but you are given credit for building a good organization.

11. *Let your people work with you, not for you.* Domination does nothing but breed "yes" men. Those who do stay on with you quickly decide to leave their initiative at home.

12. *Don't give orders if you can make your wishes known by a suggestion or a request.* People will generally produce far better work if they feel they are acting on their own than if they are ordered to do something. Then, too, they will do a better job if they know just why they have been asked to do something.

13. *Give your aides a feeling of participation by letting them in on the planning of your activities.* This tends to make them more eager because they feel they are truly a part of what is going on. Another big advantage is that some of their ideas right off the firing line may prove a big aid in the finalization of your thinking. And don't forget that the opportunity to see how a program is developed helps broaden an assistant.

14. *Show your people just what you expect of them by setting a good example.* This may mean that you will have to tighten up by making certain you are on time for appointments, that you do not take overly long, wasted lunch hours, that you don't take off to play golf when there is work to be done.

15. *Show your people that you have confidence in them by asking for their advice.* This bringing them into the big picture is a big ego builder and also gets them to work even harder than they have.

When an aide comes up with an idea, he should be heard out, even if his idea seems useless. The objective is not to discourage them from thinking of ideas. The next idea may be the one that makes a million. If the man who has this idea fears to bring it forth, it will never see the light of day.

If you want to encourage men to think, plan, and to solve problems, tell them why their ideas are adopted, and also why the idea was bypassed. Only in this way can you help your men develop.

When an idea is adopted, let its originator have the ball and run with it. He feels a personal responsibility for its development and will be a major asset to carrying out the idea.

Some executives have the ability to drop the seeds of an idea with a subordinate and let him develop it, thinking it is his own brainchild.

16. *Plan carefully what you will say before you communicate it to others.* Carelessness in the choice of words, a frown or a laugh, a yawn, a thoughtless shrug can all react to lower the morale and efficiency of those who work for you. Take care, because what you say may even cause the loss of a good man. We discussed this in Chapter 13, but it is well worth repeating here.

17. *Let your people know in advance, if you can, of anything affecting them personally.* This courtesy makes them doubly certain that they are part of the team. If changes are to be made, let them know why, so their own thinking and planning can coordinate with yours.

Cooperation at the High Levels

What we've just finished talking about is designed to help you get the cooperation and assistance of those people who work under you. Many of us also have the problem of improving coordination with others at our own level or a bit higher. Executives get better results when they know how to win the cooperation of others. This is vitally important. You can easily develop a raging set of ulcers if you run into a fight every time you want to do something.

Your ability to win the friendship and cooperation of others is an important success tool. You will have success if you have the patience, understanding, and skill to work along with others. Let's look at some of the guidelines to gaining cooperation from other people.

Perhaps first of all, be willing both to ask for cooperation and to give cooperation to others who need your help. In business there seem to be any number of people who will take assistance and then refuse to be of any help to others. There are even some who are so set and fixed in their ways that they cannot accept the help of others.

Second, be diplomatic in your dealings with other people or departments. Suppose the other department or person is causing mistakes, errors, or is lax. Your first impulse may be to accuse them of inefficiency. First count ten. They probably know they are having problems. It is needless to "expose" their weaknesses.

All you may do is gain enemies, one or more persons who will oppose your suggestions. Probably the best way for you to handle it is to suggest that they may be operating under some very difficult conditions and that you do sympathize with them. Add that you have confidence in their ability to put your suggestions in action.

When you offer a plan, prepare your own schedule and stick to it. See that the others involved have their own timetables so that they all can start immediately. It is often wise to arrange meetings so that progress can be checked. If problems seem to be popping up, see if top management will provide the extra help that is necessary to keep the program moving along on schedule.

It is often wise to have a coordinator appointed who is agreeable to all involved. It will be his job to see that everything is ready when needed. It may be unwise for you to assume the role of coordinator in some cases, because some of the others involved may object to your growing power. This is one of the problems facing an executive on the way up, and calls for diplomacy in handling all those with whom you are dealing.

Anticipate Objections

Never go into a meeting without having fully anticipated all possible objections and questions that may arise about your proposal. Sit down and note each possible objection and question and who might raise them. Then carefully plan your answers to each question. If you can anticipate which person will raise a particular question, you can develop your answer in each case to answer his objection. Diplomatic handling of the answer can often bring the other person to your side.

One thing to look out for is the older executive who may toss cold water on your proposal simply to see if you really believe in what you've said. If your proposal meets less than enthusiastic acceptance, don't appear completely disappointed and hurt. It is well to show that you can roll with the punches and come back with better ideas in the future.

What About Compromising?

Many business executives will be willing to try out a proposal, but in a limited way. If this is the case, don't reject a compromise. If your plan is good, a test will further support you. If there are any bugs in your suggestions, a small test is the best way to find what they are.

Your plan will probably stir up suggestions and ideas that may necessitate modifications. Accept them if they are good because all business growth has been a history of change and revision and compromise. If you feel that your plan is being emasculated and that the changes may cause it to fail, fight for your own ideas as hard as you can.

"Thank You" Is Vitally Important

If your proposal proves to be successful, don't take all the bows yourself. Let it be known that others were of great help. You will be able to count on their assistance in the future if they know they too benefit from your success. You can also bet that they will ask your advice and cooperation on their own projects in the future. This is the best way to get into the mainstream of operations within a company, a civic association, or any type of activity where you must live and work with others.

One quick tip here: When another person has been of help to one of your projects, take the time to write him a note, thanking him for his assistance. It's a courtesy that is not soon forgotten. If people working for another executive have been helpful, write him a note, calling this cooperation to his attention and thanking him for permitting them to work with you.

The Skills of Leadership

The ability to get people to do what you want really means the quality of leadership you possess. The man or woman who is a true leader has the ability to arouse in others the desire to follow. You can improve your leadership abilities if you are willing to develop certain skills. Let's take a look at some of the skills that a leader must possess. Very few of us possess all of them.

Be a planner. One of the prime jobs of a manager is to organize. A leader is always on top of every activity in which he is involved. He has the ability to see what must be done, and then to see that the necessary actions are carried out. He not only organizes his own time, but he also guides others so their time is most effectively utilized. And, as we have said so many other times in this book, he allows himself time to think about the future each and every day.

Make careful decisions. It is good common sense to weigh all facts carefully, to talk to all people involved, and to consider all alternatives before making a decision. This is just an extension of our discussion in Chapter 10.

Know and understand your people. It takes effort to understand just what motivates each and every one you work with and just why they act as they do. You must show a true interest in them and let them know you are interested.

Be able to communicate. An entire chapter, Chapter 13, was devoted to the importance of being able to communicate your wishes to others. All that need be said here is that you must possess the ability to explain what you want done so the other person clearly understands what is expected of him. There must be no misunderstanding.

Maintain performance standards. The ability to know and understand the job requirements of every person working for or with you is a great asset to a leader. His people become sure of what he expects from them and have confidence in their ability to produce, because they will know how they stand at all times. If you are familiar with the job description of your people, you will be better able to praise when praise should be given, to criticize when it is earned, and to provide aid and advice when they too are needed.

Ability to work with others. To obtain the cooperation of other people, you must be able to work with them without friction. This can be accomplished when your orders are eagerly accepted because others know why they are asked to do a job, and when the request has been made in a courteous manner. Your associates also appreciate it when you compliment them by asking their advice. As a result, they will go all out to assist you in reaching your goals.

Continually Practice Human Relations

The skills of good human relations can be learned just as you learn to play baseball or golf. They require that you be willing to work hard. Study yourself to find what skills need improving, and then make your plans to improve. After all, all we are talking about is another management problem—building a better executive. In this case, the finished product will be a better *you.*

The key to getting others to do what you want is to *practice* good human relations. There is a fifteen-word course in the subject. Its origin is unknown, but its meaning is certainly easy to understand and to use.

The *five* most important words are: "That was a good job."

The *four* most important words are: "What is your opinion?"

The *three* most important words are: "Will you please."

The *two* most important words are: "Thank you."

The *least* important word is "I."

17

How to Develop a Good Right Arm

A smart man can find extra time by developing a top assistant. Choosing and developing a top assistant is a vital and important step for both the owner of a business and for a corporation executive. It is also a necessity for the president of the P.T.A. and any civic club.

Why is the development of an assistant so important? First, you add hours for other managerial duties because a good assistant can take part of your workload off your shoulders. He can do some of your management tasks while you concentrate on the important job of planning future growth.

Second, you develop a man or woman who can step into your shoes in case of an accident to you, an illness, or a needed vacation.

A good assistant may also be the means of continuing a small business if the owner dies and his family wants the enterprise to continue, even though they are not capable of running it themselves.

Choosing the Right Man

The first step in developing a top assistant is to make the decision to do so. Some men have trouble here because it isn't easy for them to let go of responsibility. If the business is their own, any mistake the assistant may make is with their money.

Choosing the assistant is also a major step. If there is a relative involved, you may have little choice. But whether you choose from within your firm or family or outside, how do you know you are getting the right man?

If the person is to be promoted from inside, you have had the opportunity of observing him over a period of time. You can test him by giving him management assignments prior to his promotion. If you get the assistant from outside, give him a thorough interview. Check his references and talk with his former employers.

One important suggestion: Even though your assistant must have the same abilities as you, try to find a man who complements you. Strangely enough, two dynamic and aggressive individuals are apt to set sparks flying in a short time. The capable assistant is usually one whose strengths match your weaknesses rather than one whose strong points match yours.

Qualities of an Assistant

You cannot expect to find a well-rounded manager who is ready and willing to move in to help you. You'll have to train and work with him.

You need a man who will profit from your experience. He should be the type of person who wants to learn and can learn fast. He should be able to think and should have common sense. He must have the ability to work with people and to gain their confidence. He has to be able to lead because he will become "you" to your employees and associates—and often to your customers and suppliers.

If he has the qualities just mentioned as well as initiative, you can teach him to handle additional responsibility and authority. He can learn the skills of management, such as planning, and the supervising of others.

You might, for example, assign him the management task of hiring new employees. Learning such work will increase his understanding of the various phases of your business. The more he learns about it, the greater his satisfaction with his job. A good assistant will thrive on responsibility and a varied work routine.

How to Delegate Responsibility to an Assistant

In order to develop an assistant so he can do his best, you will have to work closely with him. In addition to personal guidance, you should lay a solid foundation for your assistant's spot in your firm.

The following suggestions can be helpful here:

Give him the facts. See that your assistant has all the necessary facts about his new responsibility. Give him a clear picture of what he is to do and how he should do it. Tell him how much responsibility he is to have. One way to start is by helping him to develop a description for his new job.

Tell him who he will be working with and personally introduce him to these people. Make certain they understand that they are to deal with your assistant and not with you in the future.

Smooth his path. Inform employees who will work with your assistant that they must cooperate with him. You can smooth his path by spelling out for them the areas of responsibility you've given your assistant. Then impress on him the importance of earning the respect of others even when he has to reprimand them.

Share your knowledge. Share your knowledge with your assistant. If he is to do a good job, you must keep him informed of your plans, their progress, and your reason for making each move. He should be warned of problems that might arise. See that he learns the ins and outs of working with other people in your firm.

An executive who fails to give his assistant such background handicaps him. By keeping him partially in the dark, the executive sells the assistant and his job short in the eyes of those with whom he must work.

Add responsibility gradually. Give your assistant additional responsibility gradually. Let him get the feel of his job. By being assigned additional responsibilities in small doses, he learns to handle new problems. Thus, he is continually absorbing additional knowledge and growing as a manager.

Hold a loose rein. Some men make the mistake of trying to keep their fingers on every move that is made in their operations. Their constant checking may make their understudies nervous and slow down their development. Rather than cause an assistant to lose confidence in himself, and sometimes his initiative, it is better to hold a loose rein.

Give him authority. Follow the management-by-exception principle when you give your man responsibility for a certain task. Give him the necessary authority to get the job done and encourage him to bring problems to you only if something seems wrong or out of line.

Train your assistant to give you one or more suggested solutions to the problems he brings to you. You then help him develop by guiding him to make the correct decision.

How Much Control for You?

When you delegate authority and responsibility to an assistant, you are using his ability to think, to plan, to act, and to evaluate. Of course, you still have to keep control. Control is important so that you can blend his progress in with the overall activities of your business.

Check regularly on assignments which you give your assistant. However, as mentioned earlier, you will want to avoid the mistake of checking on each little detail.

A word of advice here. Your assistant probably will not do the job the way you would. His approach may be as different from yours as his handwriting is different from yours. It may even be better. So long as he ethically gets the results you want, do not nag him about his methods.

Don't push your assistant onto the sidelines if you think something is going wrong. This practice tends to undermine his confidence. It also lowers his status with the employees under his supervision and with others with whom he must work.

What About Mistakes?

Everyone makes mistakes, and your assistant, without your experience and knowledge, will certainly make an occasional error. Keep in mind, though, that a smart person learns by making mistakes. Your task is to help him profit from them.

If you need to correct your assistant on a specific project, do it as we advised in Chapter 16—in private. On the other hand, always praise in public. In private, calmly discuss the mistake and point out how he can avoid the error in the future. If you are too hard on him, he may react by trying to cover up future mistakes. If this happens, you've lost communication with him and have defeated the purpose of having an assistant.

Training an Assistant

The simplest way to train your assistant is to sit down and talk with him. You explain the day-to-day running of the business, the problems you face, the principles of management he should know, and the plans and policies of your firm.

Then you turn him loose, adding management responsibilities as fast as he can assume them. Of course, you make yourself available to answer his questions.

Along with your discussions and his on-the-job practice in management, encourage your assistant to study and improve himself. He should read the trade publications in your line of business, as well as general business papers and magazines. He should also read articles and books on management subjects. One way to encourage such a program of self-development is by making the necessary books and magazines available to him.

Your assistant should also talk to suppliers' representatives and to customers in order to learn their views and needs. You can supplement this on-the-job training by using help from outside to orient your assistant. Some examples are:

Community and civic organizations. They provide a source of help, you might say, at your front door. When you encourage your assistant to participate in activities such as the Junior Chamber of Commerce, a civic club, or fund-raising drives, he gains experience in organizing projects. In these activities, he works without your guidance with citizens in your community. Many of them are your present or future customers.

Trade association conferences and conventions. A trade association is often a source of training help. Your assistant can attend a management institute if your trade association is one of those which holds them. Here your man will hear and learn from industry leaders and general business experts.

Many association convention programs devote part of their time to sessions on specific industry problems. In such meetings your assistant can gain a better insight into the overall aspect of your business. He can also make contacts with men of his own level from other firms. Such contacts can give him a source of new ideas and of solutions to problems which firms similar to yours have overcome.

Supplier training programs. Some suppliers conduct management and sales training programs for business owners and their assistants. Sometimes such programs are conducted at the supplier's office or factory. In other cases, they may be held in the field.

Administrative management courses. Your assistant can study management at a nearby school or university. In some instances, these courses are set up with the cooperation of the United States Small Business Administration. Sometimes trade associations work in conjunction with the school. Usually, the instructors are a mixture of people from the school's staff and experts from the business world. I've had the opportunity to help organize such seminars and also to teach classes at many schools throughout the nation. Generally, they've been conducted at a really high level and are excellent training grounds.

Specific Training Techniques

Some of the techniques which your assistant may be exposed to in classes and conferences which he attends are: (1) in-basket training, (2) role playing, and (3) management games. Let's briefly look at each.

In-basket training. This is a technique used to teach men and women to make decisions quickly. Your assistant is given samples of paperwork that might reach the owner's desk. He has to make a decision on each letter, memo, or report. The instructor then evaluates these decisions and suggest improvements where necessary.

Role playing. In this method of training, the assistant plays the part of his boss and deals with problems which face the top man. For instance, the assistant may have to solve the problem of suppliers who can't meet delivery dates or customers who don't pay their bills on time. Other students act out the roles of the suppliers and the customers.

Management games. With this device, your assistant gets the opportunity to practice the art of making decisions. He is given facts of a certain management situation and asked to work out an answer. Then his decision is graded. Such games give the assistant an insight into the kind of difficult situations which can crop up in business management. They also help him to learn that often there are several possible solutions to such problems. The trick is to pick the most profitable solution.

Holding a Good Assistant

After you've developed a good assistant, your big job may be that of holding him. Some businessmen don't want to take the time to train an assistant. Instead, they let you do the job and then try to hire your man. You can overcome this possibility by making it worthwhile for your assistant to stay and grow as your own job or your company grows.

Right from the start, show your assistant that the job will pay off for him and his family. Let him know what his prospects are for greater financial gain. You may want to outline your full plans for him. Or you may want to discuss only part of your expectations. If you withhold word of other rewards for various stages of his development, make sure that he has an idea that you plan to reward his efforts as your firm grows.

In some smaller firms, the added responsibility that goes with being an assistant may bring him the opportunity to buy part or all of the business in the future. I know one personable manufacturer's sales representative who was offered the second spot in a gas distributorship. Part of his pay was to be 10 per cent of the business each year for five years. His employer planned to retire after five years and in this way he was making certain that his business would continue and that he would receive both income and profits from the business. At the death of the owner and his wife (they had no children), the entire business would become the assistant's. Here was a case where a man was able to buy a business with only his labor and brains.

Whether or not this is the case in your business, the good assistant deserves good wages and has to be paid well in salary or bonus. If he isn't taken care of by one firm, often he will move on to another which does appreciate his abilities.

Developing a top assistant can pay off in many ways. It can make your own job easier, because an assistant can give you the time to plan for the future, and also to meet any emergencies that may arise.

With a competent and trusted assistant, you can take time away from your business to do things with your family. In effect, the proper assistant, after he is adequately trained and guided, can help you to live a fuller life, both at work and at home.

Your Personal Life

18

How to Gain Self-Confidence

Lack of self-confidence is one of the main bars preventing many of us from living up to our fullest potentialities. It allows fear to take over and can limit us to only a small fraction of the success we could have in our business and personal lives.

Fortunately, you can increase your self-confidence. It will take time and effort, but once you have gained it, self-confidence cannot be quickly destroyed.

What Is Self-Confidence?

Perhaps the first thing we should understand is just what this factor called self-confidence is and how we can identify it.

Self-confidence is the inner conviction that you will be able to meet and overcome every demand that is made of you. A self-confident executive acts as if success is the only possible result of any and all projects he undertakes.

This feeling will permit you to devote your fullest energies to meeting any challenge that occurs. There is no wasted effort or time spent in worrying about problems that will probably never actually arise. Ask yourself a question. How many men and women do you know who spend a good deal of time worrying about what *might* happen?

Two oil distributors serving a fast-growing suburban Midwestern area are prime examples of what self-confidence or the lack of it can do. Both knew they needed money to expand. Extra delivery trucks were needed, plant expansion was necessary. Their sales forces needed added manpower if they were to capitalize on the fast-growing market potential.

The first man was hesitant about approaching his local banker for help. He was afraid he wouldn't be able to define his needs and plans clearly. He had always depended on outside accounting help and had never taken the time to learn to read his profit and loss statement and balance sheet. He felt insecure when it came to talking about money.

In contrast, his competitor had carefully planned for his own future expansion. He knew where his business had been, where it stood at the moment, and where it could go. He went in and presented a complete prospectus to the banker.

The banker quickly arranged for local and outside financing. Today, the second man operates a business four times the size it had been when he first sought monetary assistance. His insecure competitor had failed to even hold his own against increasing competition.

Self-confidence was the answer to one distributor's success.

A large LP-Gas distributor took the trouble to build a sound group of secondary managers for his decentralized organization. When an opportunity for a merger arose, he discussed the possibilities of the merger with these aides. They convinced him that he should discard the merger plans. Today, his organization continues to grow at an even faster pace than before.

When high transportation costs worried a beer distributor, he called his drivers into conference. He explained his problems and asked for their advice. Suggestions for reroutings, call reports, and preventive maintenance techniques and plans poured out from the drivers. He remodeled his entire distribution system on these suggestions. As a result, his delivery costs have dropped well below the national average for his industry.

The Effects of Self-Confidence

Self-confidence exerts a strong effect on your organization. The man who believes in his own capacity to do the job generally believes in the ability of others to do the work assigned to them.

A confident boss helps build his organization because he builds better subordinates. He is able to delegate work and responsibility because he knows that the work will be properly done and that he will not have to worry about what is being done. He can ask and receive advice from interested, hard-working aides.

Building Self-Confidence

Self-confidence is built by successive successful experiences. You gain greater self-confidence through a series of successes in your business as well as your personal life.

The first step is to set goals for yourself. These could be personal goals such as learning how to dance, trying to stop arguing with your wife, or taking the time to teach your son to play baseball.

You can set such goals for yourself as a promotion, the success of an enterprise, improving your employee relations, or gaining a greater share of a particular market or clientele.

Setting Your Goals

Your goals should be long range. One thing particularly should be remembered here. In setting goals for the next one, five, or ten years for yourself and/or your business, remember that these goals must be reached in gradual but definite stages. This can be done by setting short-range goals to be reached in a month, six months, or one year. These shorter goals tend to act as guideposts or mileposts toward your final success. Every small success makes you feel so much more confident that you will achieve your major targets.

For instance, one oil distributor realized that he had only a small share of the potential volume gallonage that could be sold to industrial or commercial businesses. He was determined to gain a greater share of the market, and he wanted this gain by the end of the next year.

First, he surveyed the market to find the types and needs of local businesses. His next goal was to learn all he possibly could about the fuel requirements of these large prospects. Third, he readied a promotional and educational program to sell this new business.

When he had achieved his first goals, he was ready to step out after goal four, selling more gallonage to industrial and commercial prospects. His profits have risen greatly.

On Your Mark—Go!

Like the oil distributor, you have to set definite goals for yourself. Once these goals are spelled out, the big job is to get yourself moving. Getting started is in itself a hard job. Most people know their goal; but just don't know where and how to start toward it.

A proper start is often the most important ingredient in the success of any program. Actually making a start is simple if you will take the following five steps. They are simple and here they are:

1. Define the problem you must solve. What must you do and what opportunities lie ahead for you.

2. Analyze your alternatives and choose the one which offers the best opportunity for success.

3. Decide the best method to reach your goal.

4. Carefully recheck your plan and all other alternatives again to make certain you have made the wisest choice.

5. Get started. Act.

These five steps will help you overcome any indecision you may have based on any inability to organize yourself, as well as any lack of confidence in your ability to reach your goals.

How to Win the Confidence of Others

If you really want to bolster your confidence, be able to make others believe in you. When you have won the confidence of your associates, superiors, workers, customers, and the public, you have greatly built up your own ego.

There are recognized techniques that you can follow to build the confidence of others in you. Here are a few:

1. Know your business. Learn your business from top to bottom and become a recognized expert.

2. Make it easy for others to have confidence in

you. You can do this by becoming known as a person whose word is always good.

3. Build a reputation for providing good work, service and value. In this way, you gain recommendations for your business from others.

4. Set high personal standards for your everyday life. Follow the Golden Rule and treat everybody as you yourself would like to be treated.

First Impressions Are Important

First impressions are most important to help you gain the confidence of others. The four methods for getting others to believe in you just listed will help build your long-range reputation. There are also several ways to instill confidence at first sight.

1. Look and act prosperous. People find it easy to think you are on the ball if you look successful.

2. Look everyone straight in the eye. Many people believe this to be the sign of an honest man.

3. Be relaxed in the presence of others. This impression is catching and will help put others at their ease.

Sizing Up People

Another suggestion for building your self-confidence: Learn how to size up other people quickly and accurately. This is essential. When you can size up other people, you will feel more self-confident because you will be better able to sell or influence the people with whom you are dealing.

There are certain definite guides to help you size up the people with whom you'll come in contact:

1. Know what you need to know about every person that you will meet.

2. Study the person closely—his clothes, his office, home, friends, interests, mannerisms, and actions.

3. Listen to the other person. See if his ideas are well organized. Does he present them intelligently? One of the best ways to study another person is to draw him or her out by skillful questioning.

4. Ask others about the people in whom you are interested.

The Tools for Your Success

To reach your goals you are going to have to make the fullest use of all your abilities and training. And this book will help.

Read and then review the material in this book to help you improve yourself. For example, Chapter 10, "Thinking Your Way to the Right Decision," will help you decide on your primary needs and goals and how to go about achieving them. Since progress demands study, Chapters 2, 3, 4, and 5 on faster reading, learning, time management and cutting deskwork will give you the time necessary for improving your knowledge.

Because the self-confident man must be able to work at the fullest capacity, Chapters 6 and 7 on staying healthy and working under tension will prove extremely helpful. Chapters 13, 14, 15, and 16 on better writing, speech preparation and presentation, and overall communication will help you put yourself over to others.

Chapters 8 and 9 will also help you to convince others. The important ability to profit from your mistakes is also worth reviewing in Chapter 11.

Self-confidence is often the difference between major and minor successes, and even between success and failure. Your growth in business and in your personal life is so important that you must make an all-out attempt to build a more confident you.

19

Your Wife and You

Men, are you looking for a partner for your business? Maybe not. But there is someone living right in your own home who is better qualified than you realize to become not only a social asset but, perhaps, also a business asset. This secret weapon is your wife.

What I want to cover in these pages are some ways in which an executive or owner of a business can get help from his wife. Some of this assistance may never get past the front door of the home, and that's good, too—after all, many men believe a woman's place is in the home. But we'll also consider the role the wife can play in actually strengthening the business.

And every good job deserves pay of some sort so we'll consider how Mr. Husband can insure his wife's future by properly teaching her to be a widow.

But more of the serious things later. Since I'm a man, let's start with what a husband deserves in marriage. Marriage has never been considered a one-way street with the husband doing all the giving and the wife all the receiving. Simple everyday attentions can help soothe a husband's work-fevered brow.

Fisrt of all, a husband deserves to be made to feel that he is considered more than just a paycheck. There is no better way to do this than to praise his outstanding personal qualities, his taste in clothes, or his new haircut.

The little woman should hold off on her list of problems until her husband is relaxed. The last thing he wants to do is to come home to a long list of complaints. The wife should let him loosen the knots of his day before hitting him with the knots of hers.

A woman should make it her business to cheer Mr. Husband up when he is feeling low. When he's happy about some new success, he should find a good listener across the table from him and be on the receiving end of a good deal of praise.

His home should be kept in reasonable order. He should also be able to lounge around in old clothes and to dirty an ashtray without fear of criticism. A pleasing variety of good meals are also nice to come home to.

The wife should not take the enjoyment out of life by reminding her husband that he's no longer the young man he used to be. And, few men appreciate having their best story ruined by a wife reminding him that this is the fortieth time she's heard the tale.

Common courtesy requires that a man pay some attention to women at social gatherings. The last thing he wants to face is an angry scene that night at home.

Most wives seem to forget how much they like other men to be polite and gracious to them at the same affair.

If the money becomes a bit tight for a while, a man has the right to expect his wife to help tighten the belt without raising a fuss.

Few men really care if their woman is the most beautiful in town or not. After all, he picked her out and married her, didn't he? But every man has the right to expect his wife to make the effort to be always as attractive as possible.

A women wants to be treated as an equal and a man has the right to expect her to act like an adult if they have a personal disagreement. It's not hard for a man to know that his wife is turning on the tears only to get her way, even if she is wrong. The threat to withhold sex is another unfair trick.

A man has the right to the loyalty of his wife. If he and she have an argument or are making special plans about a project, he should be certain that she won't carry every intimate detail to her family or friends.

Mr. Husband may enjoy a night out with the boys once a week. It's the same thing as the P.T.A. meeting, bridge or Mahjong club, or some such activity which a woman never even gives a second thought to as she makes plans to go out on her own.

If the man likes a particular sport or has a hobby that does not interest his wife, he has a right to expect her not to needle him about it. Most men would feel just fine if their wives took up hobbies of their own.

We've just covered one dozen simple rules that will

help a man become more successful, simply because he has the kind of wonderful life that comes from being married to the kind of woman who's so nice to come home to.

Help from the Helpmate

Let's now explore further the role a woman can play to help her husband become a success in his business life. Many men have found that their wives have been secret weapons that have helped them climb the mountain of success. Women have a flair for details that men seldom possess. Once exposed to a business, many wives turn out to be the greatest asset and business partner a man possesses, even if they do not actually take part in the business.

But before you hand your wife a title and give her an office, you must find out just what kind of business talents she may have. I'm going to advocate a program to help men with their own businesses see just how well their wives really fit in. Those men working for somebody else will also find much of this of value because what we propose will help the women understand more about this world of business to which their husbands devote so much time.

Before you even mention to the little lady that you'd like her to consider taking more interest in your work, you should begin discussing some of your daily problems with her. Bring them up casually. Asking her opinion about handling certain customers is a good way to get her interested, for example. If you're having some difficulty in your dealings with a woman, you can ask your wife the best way to handle this particular customer.

If your wife seems further interested in your work, ask her if she would like to play a more active part. Many women feel they would be way beyond their depth. If that is true of your wife, it's up to you to build up her self-confidence. One of the best ways to do this is to introduce her to other women who work. Let her ask them how they like being active in business.

You may take her along to conventions or business meetings. If you do, don't send her off shopping, to a bird walk, or to a ladies tea. Invite her to sit in and listen to the discussions and speakers. Encourage her to ask questions of you and anybody else she'd like to. See that she meets other women who are taking an active role in business.

Introduce the Consultants

Next introduce your wife to your lawyer. A three-cornered session about your own long-range plans would be of great value to the wife. This session will also show her how your business will fit into your plans for your family's future. If she's like most women I know who've gotten interested in business, she'll probably start making suggestions.

How about where you work? Most of us are pretty proud of the business we have built up. We show it to others and we brag about it. If you haven't already done so, give your wife a tour of your office and other facilities. With the background she's gained by meeting others in your business, your lawyer, and your accountant, the company will mean far more to her after she's seen your base of operations.

Your partnership begins at home. Besides taking your wife down to the shop, to conventions, and to meetings with your legal and financial advisors, there are several things you can do right in your own home to give your wife a feel of the business world. Whether she ever takes any part in your business or not, this "education" will give her a broader understanding of financial matters. Perhaps this training will also help her understand why you sometimes have to say no when she asks for something that may cost a bit more than you want to spend at a particular time.

Your Home as a Classroom

Here are some of the things you can do right in your home:

1. Teach your wife to handle your family budget.
2. Let her handle the checkbook and help her to understand how important it is to keep track of the correct balance in the account.
3. Show her how to reconcile her bankbook with the monthly bank statement.
4. Let her work along with you as you fill out your income tax. If an accountant does your

forms, let your wife sit in with you when the accountant and you go over the return.

5. Let your wife plan family spending programs, such as clothing budgets, entertainment, vacations, and housing additions.

Setting Her Mind at Ease

One of the best ways to set your wife's mind at ease about the future is to introduce her to your insurance agent. She should be encouraged to work out with your agent the exact amount of monthly income she believes necessary should something happen to you. Compare this figure with the amount she could expect under your present coverages. Don't forget to call to her attention the Social Security payments she would receive.

If she feels adjustments are necessary to meet her expected needs, work these out with her. This will sharpen her interest in your business because she'll be more interested in seeing that the business grows and that her protection is greater.

Some men who have become interested in the stock market have introduced their wives to their brokers. This helps the wife gain a better understanding of the workings of the stock market. A few husbands have opened a small account for their wives and have let them learn to make their own decisions about the buying and selling of stock.

What Else Can She Do?

Now that you've gotten your wife interested in business and finances in general and your business in particular, this is a good time to step back and look at her reactions. Although it is advantageous to have a wife who is interested in your business, don't make the mistake of coaxing her to assume more responsibilities than she wishes. After all, you do not want to find that she has become primarily a business partner.

So, let's see just what a wife could do to help her husband. The most important function for her is to serve as a release for you from your work. She should arrange a balanced social life for you. It is important that you take part in social activities and not become so wrapped up in your business that her plans are continually disrupted.

Your wife can be a very valuable aide in maintaining the necessary balance that must exist between work and pleasure. If you permit her to, she'll see that you don't let your brief case become a grief case by carrying it home every night. That night at the movies for the family or the bridge game with those old friends is important relaxation for a tired businessman.

Many wives become major helpmates through their actions as sounding boards. This is a role that most women like to assume. It gives a woman the opportunity to offer a feminine opinion about problems that arise in your business, and yet, if she desires, she can still remain detached from the actual business details.

Another area in which wives can help is the business trip. If you take her along, she may be able to take advantage of shopping opportunities that you don't have time for. If there is a bargain to be had, she'll likely ferret it out, even though she is a stranger in town. In addition, with more time than you, she'll be in a position to find out about tourist attractions that will help you get more out of your trip. This outside entertainment will refresh you after a full program of business or convention activities.

Help Her Develop

One very important point to remember is that while you are on the job, you are growing intellectually. Your personality is developing and broadening. Unless your wife can develop at the same rate, she's liable to feel left behind. Eventually she might lose track of your interests and aspirations.

Help her to take whatever interest in your business she desires. Encourage her to take part in women's clubs, P.T.A., charities, or even to attend classes at schools. Have her learn to play golf so she can enjoy this sport with you. Take her along to sporting events and fishing, or at least make the offer, so she feels a part of your life.

I think you will agree that you must seek the delicate balance that is both an encouragement for her to take an interest, and also an understanding of her right to her own interests. You should not insist that your wife take more interest than she wants in your business affairs. Don't, on the other hand, let your own business life become strange to her.

The New Vice President

Now, suppose you have your own business, your wife is agreeable, and you'd like her to take a more active role. How do you start? Begin by giving her a place in your business. The first step might be to give her some company stock if you are incorporated. As a stockholder she'll be entitled to attend your annual meetings and will also take a more personal interest in the business.

When you think she is ready, make her an officer in your company. In this way you give her a recognized place, plus the added incentive that goes with the title.

Incidentally, this also paves the way for the future, should she ever have to step in and take control of the company in your absence. One wholesale food merchant's widow found that the company's only other officer was a warehouse foreman.

Give your wife a definite share of company responsibilities. These will, of course, depend on what she and you conceive of her role. Here are a few of the things she can work at:

1. You have a responsibility to help build a better community. Your wife can handle this responsibility by

working in charity drives and other community projects. Since many of these activities are directed by women, your wife should find it easy to work along with them. Your wife can be a perfect deputy to help you and your company become known as one that is community-minded.

2. Some wives have a knack of choosing premiums or giveaways that appeal to other women and children. A wife may be of great help in planning promotional programs for certain types of businesses.

3. Your wife is an excellent choice to put together social or business gatherings. Women have the social grace and experience to set these affairs up and carry them out.

This brings up another point. Keep your associates and your staff fully informed about your plans to give your wife a more active role in your business. Don't surprise them with her new authority. There is no quicker way to ruin morale and a good organization than to make it appear to your associates and subordinates that somebody is being brought in over their heads.

Keeping Her Informed

With your wife taking a more active part in your business, or at least showing a greater interest, there are many aspects of company affairs of which she should be kept informed, even though they are not her direct responsibility. There is always the chance she may have to step in to make a decision for you if you are ill or away.

Here are some of the things she should know about:

1. Tell her of your expansion plans, both short and long term. They may be only dreams, but she should still know what you have in mind.

2. Keep her up on your competitors—who they are, how they operate, who has beaten you out of business.

3. Let her know how business is, how sales are going, and if you have any trouble spots.

4. Don't keep your plans for making changes to yourself.

5. She should know where all company funds and accounts are kept.

Teach Her to Be a Widow

Every year nearly 500,000 widows are left alone in the United States. Few of them have been sufficiently prepared to face this. You owe it to your "life's partner" to make certain that she is prepared. While no man likes to think about his own death, it is good sense to do so. Death can't be avoided, but its effects on your loved ones can be cushioned by careful planning.

What would your wife do first if she suddenly had to take over and run your affairs? Would she become panic-stricken and confused by the sudden rush of events? Or would she know which way to turn, what to do? One of the most important things you can do for your wife is to give her a plan of action to follow if anything does happen to you.

Selecting a good lawyer is perhaps the most important phase of this program. Don't choose one unless you can give him your full confidence. Remember, too, that your wife will want to turn to him in your absence. Follow your lawyer's advice. He'll have suggestions about the plans you'll be making for your wife. It is a good policy not to ignore or neglect any of his suggestions.

Your plan of action is important because it will make things as easy as possible for her. This should be a written detailed plan of action. Step by step, describe every move she should make. It is also wise to give her a complete list of people she can call on for help.

This list of important people should include:

1. The name of your key employee.
2. The name, address and phone number of your lawyer.
3. The name, address, and phone number of your accountant.
4. The names, addresses, and phone numbers of your insurance agents.
5. The name of a trusted friend your wife can rely on. (This person should be told that you are depending upon him to help your wife.)
6. The names of important business contacts.

This is an important list of names. But it is also important to tell your wife where your many valuable papers and records are, especially those she would need in an emergency. Here's a list of some key papers for a wife:

1. Your insurance policies.
2. The location of your will. Make certain your will is updated and properly executed.
3. A list of banks in which you have accounts and those in which you may have safe deposit boxes.
4. Your company's key papers and records.
5. Your investment information: stocks and bonds and real estate papers, plus the name of your stock broker.
6. If you were in service, your military records.
7. Personal records, such as your birth certificate. This will be needed to claim insurance.
8. A list of your creditors and debtors and the amounts that are involved, when they are due, and how payable.
9. A list of all other assets and where they are located.

Don't Forget Money

Should anything happen to you, your wife will need money. You should open an account in her name and keep enough money in this account to meet any emergencies that could come up should something happen to you. Remember, a joint account won't do. In many states, and provinces, part of the balance is frozen upon the death of one of the codepositors.

And watch out for safe deposit boxes. If there is

anything you think your wife will need in an emergency, do not put it in a box that is registered in your name. The box may be sealed by the State upon the death of the owner. Your wife will have to go through a complicated legal proceeding to obtain papers and articles to which she is entitled and vitally needs.

You might also look into charge accounts. As Mrs. John Executive your wife has little difficulty opening any accounts. But as Mrs. Josephine Executive, widow, her credit rating may be temporarily weak. The best safeguard is to arrange charge accounts in her name at a few important stores.

With the completion of these preparations, you will have gone a long way toward giving your wife and yourself peace of mind.

20

Planning for a Happy Retirement

It is generally agreed by students of retirement that the four ingredients of a contented life in retirement are:

1. Financial security
2. Good health
3. A happy home life
4. A purpose in life

These four ingredients are usually discussed in about the order given. But they may well be better considered in the reverse order. It is wonderful to have enough money to do anything you want, but it is a complete waste of effort to accumulate this money and not know how to put it to the best use.

Money and Purpose

If you are a success in business, you are taking a big step toward financial security. You have learned the value of the dollar and the need for saving and financial planning. So, too, the getting and keeping of good health and a happy home life are "how-to's" of acquiring a happy retirement.

In the fourth ingredient—purpose—you not only have a "how" but the *why* of planning for retirement. You have the answer to the important question: "Why should I be so concerned now with the years after I retire?"

Thinking about retirement now is important because old age can come upon you gracefully—or ungracefully. How old age finds you is pretty much of your own making. Just how well you approach your old age depends upon how well you grow up physically, mentally in your general interests, and emotionally. Your attitude toward these four parts of the aging process can speed up or slow down the speed with which you grow old.

Some people reach old age intellectually the day they leave school. You've heard of people referred to as old before their time. They make no effort to solve any more problems. They are not interested in exploring new subjects or ideas. They are content to confine their reading to popular magazines, to newspaper sports pages, and to escapist literature. Some with even less interest in life become wedded to their television sets.

Yet other men stay curious about the things that go on around them. Can you think of a more exciting time to live than today? People with a purpose seek to keep up with these fascinating times. Those of us born since the turn of the century have seen almost as much progress as has happened in all the years since the earth came into being. The alert ones try their hands at studying new areas of science, or a foreign language, or enroll in some study or hobby class. This type of person can, and often does, stay intellectually alive and young at sixty and seventy and eighty. One of my friends took up the organ at sixty and became a really fine player. Another retired to a very active role in politics. He put his managerial abilities and experience to work doing some very vital work in helping his community reorganize much of its town government.

Check Your Social Habits

The years before you retire are the time to check over your social habits and to prepare yourself for the days in which all you'll have to do, perhaps, is mingle with people on a social basis. This analysis is vital because if you tend to avoid people at thirty, or forty, or fifty, you may be a hermit at sixty. On the other hand, if you make it a practice to seek people out in those early years, you'll not run short of friends later in life.

Remember also that you can't be a worrier or a hater during your youth and expect to find peace of mind at sixty-five. If a person continually complains about his minor aches and pains, tries to live in the reflection of his past glories, talks too much, or shows over-anxiety, he is often showing signs of emotional deterioration and approaching senility. It is important that you keep zip in your thinking as well as in your step.

If this seems to be a lengthy introduction to the actual planning for your retirement, it is done for a reason. It is necessary to understand why some men dread the thought of retirement, while so many of their coworkers look on it as a welcome opportunity to catch up on their hobbies, with reading, a chance to travel, and, most importantly, a time for greater companionship with their wives.

People who fear retirement may see themselves facing a period of aimless puttering while they wait to shake hands with death. These are the people who will actually devote very little time and preparation to retirement. They use all sorts of excuses for not facing up to retirement. They may see, or pretend to see, little chance that they will be able to afford retirement. If sickness or injury forces retirement, they are mentally and emotionally unprepared for it.

Plan Long in Advance

The man who is growing old in a healthy manner will make his retirement plans long in advance. This is important. Perhaps you feel that you would rather enjoy life now than to make sacrifices for an event that may seem very far off. If this is so, it is wise to consider that advance plans do not always include sacrifices.

Too often, it is the man who failed to plan ahead who must sacrifice. Many husbands and wives who have been used to country club living suddenly find that their house, their car, their friends, and their very way of life are just too expensive for them once they retire. Careful planning and investment could have assured them a comfortable standard of living.

To go a bit afield in this talk about planning: Have you ever waited too long to make a hotel reservation and found that when you got around to it there was no room? Or have you had the experience of planning a trip, a visit, or an evening out, and found that you had as much fun anticipating the event as you did at the show or on the trip?

The point being made here is that to enjoy life at any age, not just at retirement, reasonable thought and planning are needed. People who depend too much on luck seldom get what they hope for.

Assuring Your Future Security

Security in retirement is not a product which someone can manufacture and hand over to you at age sixty-five along with your retirement gift of a gold watch. Security is the fruit of years of growth, of developing your attitudes and emotions, of making personal plans.

A mature person feels secure when he finds himself able to handle the responsibilities of his everyday business life. So older people need to feel secure by reason of their own activities.

The Greatest Danger

The greatest danger to you in retirement is the loss of purpose or the reason to live. By the time most of us have reached forty, we have come to realize the importance of work in our everyday lives. Even after we retire, we must keep usefully active in order to feel that we still have a place in the scheme of things. If you acquire the feeling that nobody needs you after you have retired, you will doubtless find your old age a burden rather than a pleasure.

The idea of being able to take it easy will probably sound very enticing in your pre-retirement years. But if taking it easy merely means a routine of eating, sleeping, reading, and watching television, then you are likely to find that you are drifting into a state of unhappy idleness. Most of us need some stimulating activity to give our lives direction and purpose.

One friend retired not so long ago after fifty years "in harness." For two long years he had looked forward to the day of his retirement "when he could take things easy" and realize a life-long ambition to "travel and see." Six weeks and 10,000 miles later he was back home, with the flat statement that he had enough of driving and sightseeing. Today, this same fellow is performing the duties of acting treasurer for his church and taking pride in his new-found responsibilities.

Look for Variety

One of the important things to remember in planning for activity after your retirement is to leave a couple of doors open. The pot at the end of the rainbow that looked so good at a distance may not stand inspection at close range.

Some men in business are in a position to gradually reduce their workload as they grow older. They may, therefore, need no plan for useful activity in their old age. But others are called on to retire from full-time jobs all at once. The answer is to be ready with carefully laid out plans for doing something else when the last day on the job comes.

You may want to try your hand at operating another type of business, such as one that may be developed out of a hobby. Some businessmen with knowledge of some phase of management have founded new careers as consultants. In 1964, the United States Small Business Administration organized a group of volunteers who aided small business owners. This is called the SCORE program.

To be as successful in the retirement business as you are in your present occupation, you should carefully study all the possibilities and thoroughly plan your moves in advance.

Work Today for Tomorrow

From the standpoint of peace of mind, any activity that is not dangerous to your health is useful. There are, however, certain activities which can bring even greater rewards in self-respect and the feeling of accomplishment. The key thought here is that these activities must be engaged in before you retire so that you can set the groundwork for your after-retirement participation.

Some of the cases mentioned in this chapter show how men have successfully taken on interesting activities in such areas as civic affairs, church affairs, and politics. But they had either been involved somewhat before, or knew someone influential in the group.

The person who thinks that all he needs to do on retirement is to show an interest in civic affairs is likely to run into a stone wall of indifference. Unless you have an "in," few groups will be interested.

There is evidence that as one grows older, he is more apt to give greater attention to spiritual matters than he had in his early life. Yet, if you have rarely stepped into a church before retirement, you are not apt to find much comfort in church activities after retirement.

You may not even write that book you always planned after retirement unless you have been doing some writing before retirement. Many people feel they have a great story or two to tell. Yet, once they retire and have the time, they just don't know how to sit down in front of a typewriter and begin.

In short, you are not likely to do any of the things that look attractive to you as post-retirement activities unless you have done some of them before you stopped going to work on a regular basis.

Determine Your Values

Preparation for useful activity after your retirement requires that you spend time to determine ahead just what things are worth pursuing. With a list of objectives not dominated by human selfishness you can welcome your retirement as a time in which you will be free to work at those useful activities in which you have accumulated some experience.

You can run to retirement or you can run from retirement. And the direction you are likely to take will depend to a large extent on what useful activities have occupied your attention. And that useful means useful to society.

To retire *from* is a real tragedy. To retire *to* can mark the beginning of the most satisfying part of your entire life. I've seen a happy retirement add zest to the very life of my friends. I've seen a sparkle in their eyes and the glow of good health in their cheeks.

The major scourges of modern man are not the result of poor diet, faulty hygiene, or excessive fatigue, but to a great extent to aimless living. When the zest for living is lost, you may find senility is almost inevitable.

In addition to maintaining energy through exercises for the body, the principal need of the older people is a specific motivation—a justification for living these added years. Since positive health is more than an absence of disease, the emotional drives, personal interest and sense of values all play a key role in your daily activities.

Learn at All Ages

The trouble with old age most people find is that while the body may not function as well as it did and your bones are more apt to feel the cold, the mind still keeps working at high speed. People are capable of learning at all ages.

At age sixty, psychologists who have studied the problem say, full mental maturity is finally reached. The decline that does set in is still so slow that at the age of eighty we still have the learning ability of a 25-year-old. You can learn a foreign language, study nature, or learn of the magical words of music and art. Age is no barrier to taking up new interests and enjoying the pleasures of relaxed study. Age is no defense, therefore, against the feeling of defeat which can come from a feeling of being unwanted or unneeded.

Balanced Living

Finding a balanced way of living for a long life is not a difficult problem to solve. We need to face up to the things which block our way to finer living. Retirement has different meanings for different people. It matters chiefly what one retires to and what is in store for the future in terms of continued physical activity and satisfactory mental occupation. These factors should be studied in terms of long-range satisfactions of achievement and fulfillment.

I've heard it said that George Washington retired four times, the first time when he was only twenty-eight. Each time he became withdrawn and unhappy. He was cured by being called back into active service by his country. Benjamin Franklin retired from an everyday business life at the age of forty. As you know he lived a long and even more active and exciting life from that time on.

The Good Home Life

Ranking with your good health in importance to an enjoyable retirement is a good home life. While you are spending your days in the shop or at your office, you can usually stand the upsets at home without too much trouble. After you retire and the home becomes your full-time base of operations, the minor problems suddenly assume giant proportions.

Having a happy home life in retirement is not just a matter of getting along with your wife. There are many other important factors. For example, what changes will you make in your living arrangements? What will your housing needs be? Should you move elsewhere? We'll take a closer look at this housing problem a bit later in this chapter.

Your close proximity twenty-four hours a day may subject your marriage to new strains after retirement. You and your wife should work closely together now to plan for the later years of your life. In your joint planning, try to take into full account the interests and desires of both of you. So many men evolve all their retirement plans around their own wishes and interests. They completely forget that their wives also have the right to retire. On some points you will have to come up with a working compromise. But by knowing the possible differences in advance and having a regard for each other, you should be able to think of solutions that will be quite satisfactory for both of you.

Friends Are Necessary

One reason why many older people lose their interest in living is the lack of friends. They say they had friends once, but their friends passed on or moved away. What they are faced with is not so much the lack of friends, but the loss of friendliness. The secret of avoiding this friendless existence is to keep your interest in other people strong as you grow older. Do not let yourself be upset by the weaknesses or frailties of others.

While you are on the job, associates in your office or your industry take the place of friends to a very close degree. But once you retire, true friends are extremely necessary. The answer is to seek out and to cultivate new friends as you go along, never forgetting your old ones. Friendships do not just happen. They take cultivation and an outgoing effort.

Closely related to this problem of friendships is the problem about a place to live that was touched upon earlier. A major decision you must make is whether to move to a new community or to stay on in the old homestead. In discussing this problem with the personnel directors of companies, I've been told that perhaps half of all retirees would do well to move to another community. The other half will live quite happily in the old home town. It all depends on how much you have become attached to the old community and your neighbors.

One of the biggest reasons for moving to another area for some retirees is the change in their own neighborhood. There seems to be a definite pattern in neighborhood changes all over the country. Over a period of time the neighborhood changes from young marrieds soon with children, to a settled area with the youngsters growing up. While this is going on, some of the homes are being sold. Finally, when your own children are married and in homes of their own, you are apt to find most of the homes of your street occupied by a new influx of young marrieds, with youngsters who are apt to be annoying with their antics. Older people usually want a bit more quiet and are not that likely to remember how their own children acted. Some retirees soon acquire the reputation of crabs and their relations with the rest of their neighbors is often cold, sometimes bordering on open hostility. This is a major reason for considering a move. The other reason, of course, is that you probably no longer need the same space you did earlier.

Your Physical Well-Being

Ideally, a husband and his wife should enjoy good health. You can help assure this for your later life by taking regular physical examinations and by living wholesome, moderate lives. Strangely enough, most men seem to undergo these examinations, but few ever think of having their wives examined. Chances are many women never have a physical after childbirth unless they become quite ill.

The information in Chapters 6 and 7 will be of assistance in helping you keep yourself in good shape.

If you are healthy, normally you'll be an optimistic, well-integrated personality who will be able to find new friends wherever you go. You can secure such a personality if you practice the art of geting along with others well in advance of retirement. Now, you'll have a basketful of things to help you occupy your time.

Retirement Income

To complete the retirement ideal, you'll have a comfortable income. Here again, you must secure this in advance by making financial plans well ahead of time.

Common sense tells you that your plans for retirement should include a plan for retirement income. The extent of this income depends on your ability to save or build resources for it, and, to some degree, on what you plan to do with your life after retiring.

In any event, the sooner you begin a regular saving program, the easier it will be for you. Not only will the necessary savings be spread over a longer period of time, but compound interest will work more in your favor in reducing the effort you have to make to save sufficient money.

What of Your Business?

Your business, if you are the owner, will be an important factor in your future. Carefully managed, it may be all you need for financial security at retirement. Badly managed, it might be a white elephant which could upset your retirement plans or timing. So prudence here is as important as it is in any of the other parts of your retirement program.

If you work for somebody else, a pension plan will be a good foundation for building financial security in later life. If your company does not believe in providing pension plans for its help, you face the task of carefully planning your own retirement program. This does not mean that you have to work in the dark. You will be able to gain a great deal of advice from your banker, your insurance agent, investment advisors, and similar counselors.

I suggest you sit down in a quiet spot and outline just what you now have working for you when you retire. Then discuss this important subject with your wife and see if she has any ideas. If you feel you need a broader program, don't hesitate to take immediate action—the sooner the better. Set up a timetable, stick to it, and enjoy your later life as an active, healthy and good citizen.

Throughout this book I've tried to offer guidelines that will help you toward greater success in both your business and personal lives. This problem of a happy retirement, and it is just as important a problem as any other I have discussed, can be solved by careful planning and self-management.

If you will but make the effort to manage yourself . . . you will have all the time you need to enjoy life to its fullest.